RAISING A RESILIENT DOG

Surviving Puppyhood and Adolescence

Sally Gutteridge

ABOUT THE AUTHOR

Sally Gutteridge is a writer, trauma-informed coach, and Level 6 Dog Behaviourist with decades of experience working in the dog behaviour and training world. She is deeply passionate about ethical dog training, advocating for practices that prioritise the emotional and physical well-being of dogs, especially those who have experienced fear, anxiety, or trauma.

Sally began her journey as a dog trainer for the British Army and later worked as an instructor for Hearing Dogs for Deaf People. Over the years, she has built a wealth of experience working with thousands of dogs and their guardians. Her professional background includes founding and growing multiple successful dog education businesses, such as The International School of Canine Psychology and Behaviour (ISCP) The National Institute for Canine Ethics (NICE) and Canine Principles, which she has since taken to a place of sale.

As a qualified trauma specialist, Sally is committed to helping both dogs and humans heal from the impact of trauma. She has a profound understanding of how trauma shapes behaviour, and her work is dedicated to helping dogs live their best lives through compassionate, ethical care.

In addition to her work with dogs, Sally is an accomplished author, having written numerous books on dog behaviour and training. She is passionate about education, offering webinars, courses, and resources to dog guardians and professionals worldwide, helping them adopt a trauma-informed approach in their work.

ABOUT THE BOOK

This book gives clear guidance on the most recent and relevant research about choosing and raising a puppy, creating a successful and structured adolescence and into a resilient adult dog.

The book is science based and yet still accessible for all types of reader. It exists as a map for new and pending puppy guardians and people who are looking to help an adolescent dog feel safe and strong in the world.

There are references throughout the book and at the end, should you want to follow up on further research – but it's not compulsory, as everything you need to raise a resilient dog is right here in this book.

CONTENTS

WHY WE LOVE PUPPIES

As per developmental psychology, some qualities in puppies encourage a caregiving response in humans. According to John Bowlby, "babyness" is considered essential to human attachment patterns. In caregivers, puppies evoke a sense of protectiveness to safely explore their surroundings and have healthy growth and development. For instance, responses such as crying or whining evoke strong stimuli by the release of oxytocin which is a cuddle hormone that engenders a strong feeling to snuggle and soothe whoever is passing the stimuli.

Humans' connection with puppies dates back thousands of years and its roots stem from the domestication of wolves. The bond between humans and dogs, particularly puppies, is thought to have evolved due to its mutual benefits: humans provided food and shelter to dogs, while dogs offered companionship and protection. Modern research has found that interacting with puppies can have measurable effects on human health. For example, petting a puppy has been shown to reduce levels of cortisol which is a stress hormone and increase the production of oxytocin, a hormone linked to bonding and affection (Beetz et al., 2012). This interaction builds an emotional connection and helps reduce stress, anxiety, and even symptoms of depression.

In addition to the emotional benefits, puppies also offer physical advantages. Dog guardianship has been associated with increased levels of physical activity, as dogs require regular walks, playtime, and attention. This increased physical activity can lead to improved cardiovascular health, weight management, and overall fitness (Cutt et al., 2008). Additionally, studies have demonstrated that the presence of dogs in a household can lower blood pressure and cholesterol levels and contribute to improved long-term health outcomes (Allen et al., 2002). The joy that puppies bring into people's lives extends beyond the individual level. Puppies have been known to encourage social interactions, especially in urban environments where people can sometimes feel isolated. Walking a dog in public spaces often leads to conversations with strangers, increasing socialisation and creating a sense of community (McNicholas et al., 2005).

Understanding the development of puppies involves more than just observing their behaviours; it requires a solid grasp of the science behind their growth, learning processes, and health needs. The purpose of this book is to explore these scientific aspects while offering practical advice for dog guardians and aspiring puppy parents. The science of puppy development encompasses a range of disciplines, from genetics and biology to psychology and ethology. Researchers have identified several critical stages in a puppy's development, each characterised by specific physical, cognitive, and emotional milestones. The intersection of science and practical advice makes puppy guardianship more rewarding and contributes to the creation of healthier, happier dogs.

The critical period of socialisation typically occurs between 3 and 14 weeks of age. During this time, puppies are especially receptive to learning about the world around them. They become more attuned to human interactions, other animals, and environmental stimuli. Proper socialisation during this period is crucial for preventing behavioural issues such as aggression or fearfulness later in life (Wright, 2018). In addition to socialisation, another important area of puppy development is training. Puppies are naturally curious and eager to learn, making them highly responsive to positive reinforcement techniques. Scientific research has shown that puppies have an impressive ability to learn commands and behaviours through reinforcement, with the most effective methods involving reward-based training (Pryor, 2002).

Health and nutrition are also integral to a puppy's development. Proper nutrition during the formative months is essential for healthy growth and development, particularly in terms of muscle, bone, and brain development (Wysong, 2008). Research on canine nutrition emphasises the importance of a balanced diet that provides the necessary nutrients, vitamins, and minerals (Case et al., 2011).

Knowing the science behind canine behaviour allows guardians to address behavioural issues more effectively. By understanding why puppies behave the way they do and the factors that influence their actions, guardians can use science-based strategies to manage undesirable behaviours. For instance, behaviour problems such as chewing, barking, and digging can often be traced back to a lack of mental stimulation or anxiety. Guardians can mitigate these issues by providing puppies with proper training, exercise, and enrichment activities that meet their physical and mental needs (Miller, 2009).

The emotional bond between puppies and their guardians plays a vital role in the dogs' happiness and well-being. Research has demonstrated that positive human-animal interactions lead to increased levels of oxytocin, the "love hormone," in both dogs and their guardians (Odendaal, 2000). This hormonal response contributes to feelings of affection, trust, and attachment, reinforcing the bond between humans and puppies. By developing a loving, supportive environment, guardians can ensure that their puppies grow up to be emotionally well-adjusted, leading to healthier, happier dogs

CHAPTER 1
CONCEPTION AND GENETICS

Genetics is a branch of biology that deals with genetic information and its transfer to upcoming generations. In a broader sense, genetics cover how genes are transferred, how they are structured in cells, regulate and interact with their environment and with each other. The process through which puppies come into existence consists of a series of events. The process starts with the mating of a male and female dog which leads to the conception of a new life. Genetics determine everything related to the coat, colour, texture, behaviour, predisposition and health of the newborn puppy. Specific traits are inherited from the parents to have distinct characteristics and features of the puppy and contribute to a variety of dog breeds.

The Basics of Genetics, Inheritance and Breed Traits

Genetics is the study of how traits are passed from parents to offspring. These traits are encoded in DNA, the molecular blueprint of life. The transmission of genetic information follows specific patterns, often referred to as Mendelian inheritance, named after Gregor Mendel, the scientist who established the foundational principles of genetics in the 19th century. According to Mendelian inheritance, offspring inherit one set of chromosomes from each parent, resulting in two sets of chromosomes (diploid). These chromosomes contain genes that influence the traits the offspring will exhibit.

Each gene can exist in different forms called alleles, which can be dominant or recessive. Dominant alleles mask the effects of recessive alleles when both are present in the same gene pair. For example, if a dog inherits a dominant allele for black fur and a recessive allele for brown fur, the dog will have black fur because the dominant black fur allele overrides the recessive brown fur allele. Puppies similarly inherit their genetic makeup. The male dog contributes sperm, carrying half of the genetic information, and the female dog provides the egg, which also carries half of the genetic material. The sperm and egg combine during fertilisation to form a zygote, a single cell that contains a full set of chromosomes, half from each parent. This zygote undergoes cell division and differentiation to eventually become a fully developed puppy.

Breed traits are the physical and behavioural characteristics that distinguish one breed of dog from another. These traits are largely determined by the specific genetic makeup of the breed, shaped over generations by selective breeding. Selective breeding is the practice of mating dogs with desirable traits to produce offspring that exhibit those same traits. Over time, this practice results in the establishment of distinct dog breeds, each with a characteristic set of physical traits, behaviours, and temperaments.

For instance, the size, shape, and colour of a dog's coat are all genetically controlled. The Labrador Retriever is known for its water-resistant coat, which is an adaptation to the breed's origins as a working dog in waterfowl hunting. The genetic basis for the Labrador's coat type is linked to specific alleles that regulate the development of fur texture and the production of oils that make the coat water-resistant. Similarly, the Poodle's curly coat is another breed-specific trait, controlled by a different set of genes, which gives the breed its distinct appearance. In addition to physical traits, breed-specific behavioural tendencies are also genetically determined. For example, Border Collies are known for their exceptional intelligence and herding instinct, while Dachshunds are bred for hunting and have a strong prey drive. These behaviours are also products of the genes inherited from their parents, shaped by the selective breeding practices that prioritise certain traits.

Furthermore, the genetic basis of certain health conditions is also breed-dependent. Some dog breeds are more prone to specific genetic disorders, which have been documented through extensive research. For example, large breeds like the Great Dane and German Shepherd are more prone to hip dysplasia, while the Cavalier King Charles Spaniel is often affected by heart issues such as mitral valve disease. These breed-specific genetic vulnerabilities are inherited according to the same principles of Mendelian inheritance.

Genetic variability refers to the differences in genetic makeup between individuals within a population. In dogs, genetic variability is essential for maintaining a healthy and robust gene pool. However, selective breeding practices can sometimes lead to reduced genetic diversity, especially in purebred dogs. Inbreeding, or mating between closely related dogs, can result in a higher risk of genetic disorders and a loss of beneficial traits. Therefore, maintaining genetic diversity is crucial for the long-term health of dog breeds. Breeders often aim to balance the desire for specific traits with the need for genetic diversity to reduce the risk of inherited health problems. In addition, genetic testing and the use of outcrossing can help mitigate the negative effects of inbreeding and improve the overall genetic health of the breed.

The Role of Selective Breeding

Selective breeding involves choosing parent dogs with specific traits to produce offspring with similar characteristics. For example, breeders may select dogs with a particular coat colour, size, or temperament to create puppies that meet breed standards. Over time, this results in distinct breeds with identifiable traits that set them apart from others. For working breeds such as Border Collies, selective breeding has led to an exceptional level of intelligence and herding instinct, while companion breeds like the Cavalier King Charles Spaniel have been bred for a gentle and affectionate temperament. Breeding for specific traits, particularly physical appearance, has shaped many of the popular dog breeds we recognise today. Purebred dogs are often subject to rigorous standards set by kennel clubs, with detailed descriptions of the acceptable traits for each breed. These standards focus on characteristics such as coat texture, colour, size, and conformation (the shape of the dog's body). In some cases, specific behaviours are also encouraged, such as the alertness of the German Shepherd or the calm nature of the Shih Tzu.

1. **Impact on Health**

One of the most significant concerns with selective breeding is its potential negative impact on the health of dogs. By narrowing the genetic pool, selective breeding can increase the risk of inherited health problems. When only a small group of dogs is used for breeding, genetic disorders can become more prevalent. Many pedigree dogs suffer from genetic disorders because they have been bred from a limited gene pool, which can lead to the expression of harmful recessive traits. For example, the bulldog, a breed that has been selectively bred for a short snout, often suffers from brachycephalic airway syndrome. This condition causes difficulty in breathing, overheating, and associated health complications.

Similarly, large breeds such as the Great Dane are prone to hip dysplasia, a genetic condition that affects the development of the hip joint, leading to arthritis and pain in the later stages of life. Other breeds, such as the Cavalier King Charles Spaniel, are predisposed to heart diseases like mitral valve disease, which can be exacerbated by selective breeding practices that emphasise conformation over health. Research by O'Neill et al. (2014) has shown that the increasing prevalence of inherited diseases in certain breeds is largely due to selective breeding practices. The desire for particular traits, such as a specific coat colour or facial structure, has often taken precedence over the health and welfare of the dog. This has led to the widespread occurrence of conditions like cataracts, hip dysplasia, and epilepsy, which are now common in many breeds.

2. Impact on Behaviour

Selective breeding also plays a significant role in shaping the behaviour of dogs. Breeds are often selected for particular temperaments and behavioural traits that align with human needs. For instance, herding dogs like Border Collies and Australian Shepherds are bred for intelligence, trainability, and a strong work ethic, while toy breeds such as the Chihuahua are often bred for companionship and are typically small, lively, and affectionate. However, the pursuit of specific behavioural traits through selective breeding can sometimes have unintended consequences. Some breeds, particularly those bred for guarding or hunting, may develop aggressive tendencies if not properly socialised or trained. For example, certain guarding breeds like the Rottweiler and Doberman Pinscher, while known for their loyalty and protective instincts, can exhibit aggression if not properly managed. This can lead to behavioural problems such as excessive territoriality, fear-based aggression, or a heightened prey drive.

Selective breeding may also lead to a lack of genetic diversity, which can exacerbate behavioural problems. Limited genetic variation can result in a higher prevalence of undesirable traits, such as excessive shyness or hyperactivity. Additionally, the focus on certain behavioural traits can sometimes lead to the exaggeration of these traits and may result in imbalanced or problematic behaviours. For instance, a dog bred to be highly energetic and driven may struggle to adapt to life in a more sedentary environment, potentially leading to anxiety or destructive behaviours.

Chapter Highlights

- Genetics determine key traits like coat, colour, behaviour, and health of puppies, inherited from their parents through Mendelian inheritance.

- Selective breeding shapes distinct dog breeds, but it can also increase the risk of genetic disorders and health problems due to reduced genetic diversity.

- Selective breeding influences dog behaviour, with some breeds predisposed to specific temperaments or tendencies, which may cause unintended behavioural issues if not properly managed.

CHAPTER 2

IN THE WOMB

The period of gestation is typically nine weeks and during this time, a lot of changes take place within the female dog body. Once the puppy is safely born, he or she goes through growth and development to grow further. After the mating takes place, a single cell fertilises the egg. Once the egg is fertilised, the nine-week journey of the future puppy starts.

Puppy Development Stages in Utero

The stages of development during this period are essential to understanding the physiological and anatomical changes that occur in the formation of a puppy. These stages dictate the growth and development of the puppy's organs and systems and also play a key role in shaping its future behaviour and health.

1. Stage: Fertilisation and Early Cell Division

The first stage of development begins with fertilisation. During this process, the male dog's sperm fertilises the female dog's egg, forming a zygote. This fertilised egg contains all the genetic material needed for the development of a new dog, inheriting half of the genetic material from each parent. Shortly after fertilisation, the zygote begins to divide rapidly through mitosis, forming a ball of cells. These cells continue to divide as they travel down the fallopian tube toward the uterus.

As the zygote reaches the uterus, it becomes a blastocyst, a hollow sphere of cells. The blastocyst begins to implant itself into the uterine wall, where it will receive nourishment and continue developing. During this early period, there is no visible sign of pregnancy, and the embryo is just a tiny cluster of cells that is growing and dividing at a rapid pace.

2. **Stage: Embryonic Development**

By day 10 to 12, the embryo undergoes a critical process of organ development known as organogenesis. This is when the basic structures of the body begin to take shape. The heart, brain, and spinal cord begin to form, and the rudimentary digestive system starts developing. The embryo is now growing rapidly, and its cells are beginning to specialise in the tissues that will form its organs and systems. At this point, the developing embryo is around the size of a pea.

During the embryonic stage, the puppy's nervous system starts to take shape. The neural tube, which will eventually develop into the brain and spinal cord, begins to form. The heart begins to beat by the end of this stage, and the circulatory system starts to develop, enabling the embryo to receive nutrients from the mother via the placenta. The placenta is a vital organ in pregnancy, responsible for providing oxygen and nutrients to the growing puppy while also removing waste products.

By day 20 to 21, the puppy's limbs start to form, and the beginnings of facial features such as the eyes and ears begin to emerge. At this stage, the developing embryo is referred to as a foetus, marking the transition from early embryonic development to more advanced stages of growth.

3. **Stage: Foetal Development**

During the foetal stage, which lasts from approximately day 22 to day 45, the puppy's body starts to take on a more recognisable form. The major organs and systems that were initially formed begin to develop further, and the puppy begins to grow at a faster rate. By around day 25, the heart is fully formed, and the circulatory system is well established. The digestive system continues to develop, and the kidneys begin functioning to filter waste products.

At this stage, the development of the facial features continues, with the formation of the eyelids, nose, and mouth. The ears become more distinct, although the puppy is still unable to hear. The first signs of fur growth begin to emerge, although the coat is still sparse and underdeveloped. By day 35, the foetus is visibly growing larger, and bones are starting to form. The skeletal structure of the puppy takes shape, and cartilage begins to harden into bone. The nervous system continues to mature, and the puppy's movements become more coordinated. The foetus can now move its limbs, and by day 40, it is capable of some limited movements within the uterus, though these movements are still subtle.

4. **Stage: Late Foetal Development**

The final stages of development, from day 46 to day 58, see significant growth in the foetus, and the organs continue to mature. At this point, the puppy is developing more distinct features, such as a more developed coat, fully formed ears, and eyelids. The eyes remain closed, and the ears remain sealed, as the puppy's sensory organs are still not fully functional.

During this stage, the foetus gains weight rapidly. The internal organs are now fully formed, and the brain continues to develop. The puppy starts accumulating fat, which will be important for thermoregulation after birth. The coat begins to become more apparent, and fur is starting to develop more fully across the puppy's body. The digestive system is fully functional, and the puppy begins to swallow amniotic fluid, which helps stimulate the development of the gastrointestinal tract. As the puppy's organs mature, its senses also begin to develop. While the eyes are still closed, the puppy can begin to sense light through its eyelids. The sensory systems, including touch, taste, and smell, are functioning more effectively, although the puppy is still largely dependent on the mother's placenta for oxygen and nutrients. By the end of this stage, the puppy is almost fully developed and prepared for birth. The bones have become more solid, and the muscles are stronger. The puppy's nervous system is more coordinated, and its body is approaching its final size before birth.

5. **Stage: Pre-Labour and Birth**

In the final days before birth, the puppy undergoes rapid growth, and its body prepares for life outside the womb. The internal organs mature further, and the brain undergoes final development, preparing the puppy for postnatal life. The foetal position becomes more stable, with the puppy positioning itself head-down in preparation for birth.

The mother's body begins to prepare for the delivery process as well. Hormones such as oxytocin help the uterus contract, and the cervix begins to dilate. The amniotic sac, which has been providing the puppy with protection and fluid, begins to rupture, signalling the onset of labour. At this stage, the puppy is fully developed and ready to be born, marking the end of the development process in the womb. Birth typically occurs around day 63 of pregnancy, although it can vary depending on the breed and the individual dog.

Maternal Health and its Effects on Puppy Development

The overall health of the dam is paramount for the proper development of the unborn puppies. Any pre-existing health conditions or illnesses experienced by the mother during pregnancy can have adverse effects on the puppies. In particular, infections, endocrine imbalances, and chronic diseases can compromise the development of the foetuses, leading to complications such as low birth weight, organ malformations, or even premature birth.

Research has shown that maternal diseases like diabetes, kidney disease, and heart conditions can influence the growth and health of puppies. For instance, maternal diabetes, whether pre-existing or gestational, can result in large puppies, a condition known as macrosomia, which can complicate the delivery process. Furthermore, the puppies may also be more prone to developing diabetes later in life (Vanand et al., 2020). Similarly, infections such as parvovirus, distemper, or toxoplasmosis can cause birth defects, stillbirths, or congenital diseases in puppies. Ensuring that the dam is healthy, vaccinated, and free from infections is critical in reducing the risks of developmental issues.

Additionally, chronic stress or malnutrition can exacerbate these health issues, further compromising the developmental environment for the puppies. Maternal health, therefore, forms the foundation for a healthy pregnancy and optimal outcomes for the puppies.

1. **The Role of Maternal Stress**

Stress is an inevitable part of life, but excessive or chronic stress in a pregnant dog can have profound effects on the developing puppies. Stress can affect a dog at various levels—physiologically, behaviourally, and hormonally. Chronic stress in pregnant dogs can lead to an increase in stress hormones, particularly cortisol. Cortisol is known to cross the placenta and directly affect the foetus, potentially leading to developmental delays, abnormal growth patterns, and behavioural disorders.

Studies have shown that elevated levels of cortisol in pregnant animals can lead to adverse pregnancy outcomes such as low birth weight, impaired immune system development, and behavioural disturbances in offspring. Research in humans has similarly shown that maternal stress can result in neurodevelopmental disorders and increased vulnerability to diseases in children (King et al., 2015). In dogs, stress-induced behavioural issues, such as anxiety, fearfulness, and aggression, have been linked to prenatal stress exposure (Meaney et al., 2007).

In addition to the direct effects of cortisol, maternal stress can also lead to the reduction of blood flow to the uterus, impairing the supply of oxygen and nutrients to the developing puppies. This restricted blood flow can hinder foetal development, resulting in smaller puppies or, in extreme cases, stillbirth. It is therefore essential for the dam to be in a calm and stable environment throughout pregnancy. Minimising stressors, such as loud noises, unfamiliar environments, and changes in routine, can help create a more favourable developmental environment for the puppies.

2. Maternal Nutrition and its Impact on Puppy Development

Nutrition during pregnancy plays a crucial role in the health of both the dam and her puppies. A balanced and appropriate diet ensures that the dam receives the essential nutrients needed for her own health, as well as the proper nutrients to support the developing puppies. Poor maternal nutrition can lead to a variety of complications, including low birth weight, developmental delays, and an increased risk of birth defects.

A dog's nutritional needs during pregnancy are increased, particularly in the later stages of gestation when the puppies are growing rapidly. The demand for protein, energy, vitamins, and minerals rises significantly. Protein is essential for the development of the puppies' tissues and organs, while carbohydrates and fats provide the necessary energy for growth. Deficiencies in these essential nutrients can lead to a variety of problems, including underdeveloped organs, weakened immune systems, and poor coat conditions.

Research has shown that the balance of omega-3 and omega-6 fatty acids in a dog's diet can also influence puppy development. Omega-3 fatty acids, which are found in fish oil and certain seeds, are known to support brain development, particularly the development of the central nervous system. Studies have indicated that puppies born to dams with adequate levels of omega-3 fatty acids show better cognitive development and reduced stress responses compared to those born to dams with insufficient levels (Baker et al., 2018). Micronutrients, such as calcium and iron, are also critical during pregnancy. Calcium is necessary for the development of strong bones and teeth, while iron is essential for the formation of red blood cells. Iron deficiency in the dam can lead to anaemia, which can reduce the oxygen supply to the puppies and affect their development. Similarly, a lack of folic acid can lead to neural tube defects and other developmental problems.

Excessive or insufficient calorie intake can also have long-term consequences on puppy development. Obesity in pregnant dogs has been linked to an increased risk of stillbirths, premature birth, and complications during delivery. Conversely, malnutrition or a lack of adequate calories can result in smaller puppies, lower birth weights, and an increased risk of hypoglycaemia after birth (McGreevy et al., 2005). The nutritional care of the dam is essential not only for her own health but also for the health of her puppies. Ensuring that the dam receives a balanced diet, rich in essential nutrients, supports optimal foetal development and prepares the puppies for a healthy start to life.

Chapter Highlights

- Pregnancy in dogs involves distinct stages: fertilisation, embryonic, foetal, and late foetal development, each crucial for organ and system formation.

- Maternal health, stress, and nutrition significantly impact puppy development, with poor nutrition or stress leading to complications like low birth weight or behavioural issues.

- Selective breeding can lead to reduced genetic diversity, affecting both the health and behaviour of puppies due to inbreeding.

CHAPTER 3

BIRTH AND THE NEONATAL STAGE

After birth, till they are 2 weeks old, puppies completely rely on their mother to provide them with food and cleanliness. The senses of smell and touch are present after birth. However, they have limited ability to move and can crawl slowly. Understanding this stage helps caregivers to provide essential nutrients that can contribute to healthy development. Behaviourally, when puppies are born, their eyes are normally closed. The newborn puppy makes his way to his mother and food source using its sense of smell and touch. They spend most of their time sleeping in the early stages.

What Happens During Birth

Understanding what happens during birth and the neonatal stage can help ensure proper care for the puppies and dams and contribute to a smoother delivery and a healthy start for the puppies.

1. **Stage: Preparation for Labour**

The first stage of labour is often the longest and may last anywhere from six to twelve hours, although this can vary depending on the individual dog and the size of the litter. During this stage, the dam will exhibit signs of restlessness, panting, and nesting behaviour. She may seek a quiet, comfortable place to give birth, and the guardian or breeder needs to ensure a clean and secure area is provided. The onset of labour is triggered by hormonal changes in the dam's body. As the pregnancy nears its end, the hormone progesterone drops, and this decrease is essential for the onset of labour. Concurrently, oxytocin, a hormone responsible for stimulating uterine contractions, begins to rise. These hormonal shifts lead to the softening and dilation of the cervix, preparing the dam for the delivery of the puppies. During this first stage, the dam may experience mild uterine contractions as her body begins to prepare for the more intense contractions of the second stage.

2. **Stage: Active Labour and Delivery**

Stage two of labour is the stage of active delivery, where the puppies are born. This stage typically lasts anywhere from two to six hours, depending on the number of puppies and the dam's characteristics. Uterine contractions become stronger and more frequent, pushing the puppies towards the birth canal. The dam may vocalise, pant heavily, and exhibit further signs of distress as the puppies begin to move through the cervix and into the birth canal.

Once the first puppy is positioned in the birth canal, the dam will begin to push. The muscular contractions of the uterus force the puppy out, and the birth process is complete when the puppy is delivered into the world. The presence of amniotic fluid and the umbilical cord is common at birth, and it is the dam's instinct to chew through the cord and clean the puppy to stimulate its breathing. Each puppy is typically born within 30 to 60 minutes of the previous one, though there may be periods of rest between deliveries. The dam may exhibit some restlessness during this time but will typically remain focused on delivering the puppies. It is important to note that the dam's behaviour during labour is usually a good indication of the progression of delivery, with excessive distress potentially indicating complications.

3. Stage: Expulsion of the Placenta

After each puppy is delivered, the placenta follows shortly thereafter. The placenta, which has been providing oxygen and nutrients to the developing puppies throughout pregnancy, is expelled from the dam's body. It is important to ensure that the dam expels all placentas, as retained placentas can lead to infection or other complications. The dam will usually eat the placenta, as this provides her with nutrients that help her recover after the strenuous delivery process. The expulsion of the placenta can be considered a continuation of stage two, but it is often viewed as stage three of the birth process. The delivery of the placenta ensures that all of the puppies' nutrients have been cleared from the dam's uterus, and the reproductive system begins to return to its normal state.

4. Neonatal Stage: The First Few Days

Following the birth, the neonatal stage begins. This is the period of time immediately after birth during which the puppies are highly dependent on the dam for nourishment, warmth, and protection. The neonatal stage lasts for the first two weeks of a puppy's life, during which time the puppies undergo significant growth and development.

At birth, puppies are blind, deaf, and helpless, relying entirely on the dam for survival. They instinctively begin to nurse from the dam's teats, as the sucking reflex is fully developed at birth. Colostrum, the first milk produced by the dam, provides essential antibodies that help protect the puppies from infections during the first few weeks of life. It is crucial that puppies receive adequate colostrum within the first 24 hours of life to ensure proper immune system development (Merck Veterinary Manual, 2014).

During the neonatal period, puppies also rely on their dam for warmth. Newborn puppies are unable to regulate their body temperature effectively, and the dam's body heat, along with the warmth of the nest, helps to keep them comfortable. Inadequate warmth can lead to hypothermia, a condition that can be fatal for puppies. The dam's attentiveness during this stage is vital to ensuring the puppies stay warm, fed, and comfortable. As the puppies grow, they will begin to open their eyes around ten to fourteen days after birth. Their sense of hearing also begins to develop, and they will start to respond to sounds and movements. At this stage, they begin to show signs of playfulness, although they are still largely dependent on the dam for survival.

5. **Complications During Birth**

While the birth process is generally straightforward, complications can arise. Prolonged labour, where the dam struggles to deliver the puppies, can result in foetal distress or maternal exhaustion. In some cases, puppies may become lodged in the birth canal, requiring veterinary assistance. Dystocia, or difficult birth, can also occur if the puppies are too large for the dam's birth canal or if the position of the puppies is abnormal. In such cases, veterinary intervention may be necessary, including the use of forceps, caesarean sections, or medications to help facilitate the birth process. Breeders or guardians need to monitor the dam closely during labour and be prepared to seek veterinary assistance if complications arise.

The first two weeks of a puppy's life are critical to its development, as they lay the foundation for its sensory abilities, physical health, and overall well-being. During this period, puppies are completely dependent on their mother (the dam) for everything, including warmth, nutrition, and socialisation. Sensory development during these early days is essential for establishing healthy physiological systems, as well as for shaping the behavioural and emotional development of the puppies. Among the most important factors influencing a puppy's growth in the neonatal stage are touch, warmth, and nutrition, which are all closely intertwined in the overall development process.

Sensory Development in the First Two Weeks and the Importance of Nutrition

At birth, puppies are highly undeveloped. Their sensory systems are not fully functional, and they rely heavily on their sense of touch and the comfort provided by their mother. Over the first two weeks, puppies undergo a rapid transformation, as their sensory systems gradually mature, enabling them to interact with their environment and begin to learn from their surroundings.

1. **Vision and Hearing**

Puppies are born blind and deaf, with their eyes and ears sealed shut. Vision and hearing develop progressively during the first few weeks of life. At around ten to fourteen days, the puppies' eyes begin to open, but their vision remains blurry for some time. Initially, they can only perceive light and dark, and it takes several weeks before they can focus on objects. Hearing also develops in a similar timeline. Puppies are born without the ability to hear, but by the time they are around two weeks old, their ears begin to open. As their hearing develops, they become more responsive to sounds, particularly the sounds produced by their mother, such as her vocalisations or the noises associated with nursing. Sound plays a vital role in their ability to interact with their environment and their mother, forming the basis for later social behaviour and communication skills (Liu et al., 2017).

2. Touch

Touch is the most important sensory system during the first few days of a puppy's life. Newborn puppies use their sense of touch to navigate and orient themselves, particularly when searching for their mother's teats for feeding. This sense of touch is also crucial for bonding and attachment, as puppies rely on physical contact with their mother for warmth and security. The act of licking and being licked by the dam is an essential part of this process, as it not only provides tactile stimulation but also helps with hygiene and blood circulation in the puppies. The importance of touch extends beyond the dam's care. Puppies that are handled by humans during the neonatal stage, particularly gently and positively, can develop better social skills and emotional stability as they grow. Research has demonstrated that early tactile interactions can enhance puppies' emotional resilience and adaptability (Bateson, 2004).

3. The Role of Warmth

Newborn puppies cannot regulate their body temperature independently, which makes warmth a critical factor for their survival and health in the first two weeks. The dam's body provides the primary source of warmth, as the puppies cluster together near her abdomen to stay warm. Hypothermia is a serious risk for puppies in the neonatal period, and without proper warmth, they can become lethargic, weak, and unable to nurse effectively.

Maintaining a warm, stable environment is essential for puppies during their first few weeks. If the ambient temperature is too low, puppies can lose heat quickly, and this can lead to serious health issues such as respiratory distress or even death. A puppy's temperature regulation system is still immature at birth, which means they require external heat sources to maintain their body temperature. In the absence of the dam, breeders or pet guardians need to ensure that puppies are kept in a warm, safe environment, typically between 29°C and 32°C (84°F and 90°F) during the first few days, gradually decreasing to around 26°C (79°F) by the end of the second week (Merck Veterinary Manual, 2020).

4. The Importance of Nutrition

During the first two weeks, the most critical nutritional source for puppies is the dam's milk. Colostrum, the first milk produced by the mother, is particularly vital, as it contains high levels of antibodies, which help to protect the puppies from infections in the early stages of life. Colostrum is rich in immunoglobulins, which are essential for building the puppies' immune system, as puppies are born with little to no immunity of their own (Breen et al., 2017). As the puppies grow, the dam's milk continues to provide essential nutrients, including proteins, fats, and carbohydrates, which are necessary for their rapid growth. Puppy milk replacers can be used if the dam is unable to nurse or if there are concerns about the quantity of milk available, but the nutritional formula must be appropriate for the age and size of the puppies.

Feeding frequency is also a critical consideration. During the first week, puppies generally need to nurse every two hours, even through the night. By the second week, they may begin to sleep longer between feedings, but it is still essential that they receive regular nourishment to support their rapid growth. Puppies that do not receive adequate nutrition during this period may experience stunted growth, weakness, or dehydration, which can result in severe health complications.

Chapter Highlights

- Labour involves three stages: preparation, active delivery, and expulsion of the placenta, with the dam showing signs of restlessness and nesting.

- Newborn puppies rely on their mother for warmth, food, and hygiene, being unable to regulate body temperature or move effectively.

- The neonatal stage is crucial for sensory development, with puppies initially relying on touch, and later developing vision and hearing by two weeks.

- Colostrum is vital for puppies, providing antibodies that protect them from infections and supporting immune system development in the first 24 hours.

- Warmth and proper nutrition are critical for puppy survival; inadequate care can lead to hypothermia, stunted growth, and other health issues.

CHAPTER 4
THE EARLY LEARNING WINDOW

When puppies are in the early phase of development, they are highly sensitive to their environmental stimuli. Interacting with their environment helps shape their behaviour and temperament. The early learning window phase which necessitates the development of social skills and stress management spans approximately three to fourteen weeks of the puppy's age.

Critical Socialisation Periods

When there is an increased neural plasticity, it indicates high socialisation which helps the puppy to become receptive to external stimuli. Going through socialisation helps build social competence and emotional resilience (Freedman and Scott, 1966).

1. **Maternal Influence**

Maternal interactions form the cornerstone of early learning in puppies. Beyond providing essential nutrition and immunological protection, the mother's behaviour plays a pivotal role in the modulation of the offspring's stress responses. Through activities such as grooming, nursing, and responsive care, the mother establishes a secure base that encourages safe exploration of the environment. Empirical evidence demonstrates that consistent maternal care can attenuate stress reactions and promote balanced emotional development (Zanghi and Rodda, 2013).

Variations in maternal style have also been linked to differences in offspring temperament. For example, mothers who exhibit consistent nurturing behaviours tend to produce puppies with lower anxiety levels, whereas irregular or inconsistent care can predispose puppies to later-life behavioural instability. This association suggests that maternal behaviours not only offer immediate comfort but also influence the programming of neural circuits governing future adaptive responses (Zanghi and Rodda, 2013).

2. Littermate Interactions

Interactions with littermates are integral to the acquisition of essential social skills. Through structured play, competition, and occasional conflict, puppies learn to modulate their behaviour and understand complex social cues. These early peer interactions facilitate the development of bite inhibition, communication signals, and the recognition of social hierarchies. Studies indicate that puppies involved in frequent and dynamic littermate play exhibit greater social adaptability and a reduced tendency towards fear-based responses (Morello et al., 2015).

Furthermore, the opportunities for early conflict resolution that arise during these interactions enable puppies to navigate hierarchical relationships and discern appropriate behavioural boundaries. The absence or paucity of such interactions may lead to difficulties in establishing social norms when encountering unfamiliar peers later in life (Morello et al., 2015).

3. Environmental Stimuli

The sensory environment in which puppies are reared plays an influential role in cognitive and behavioural development. Exposure to a diverse range of stimuli—encompassing varied sights, sounds, textures, and spatial configurations—encourages exploratory behaviour and fosters cognitive flexibility. Research has shown that controlled exposure to a broad array of environmental cues during the sensitive period can diminish the likelihood of developing maladaptive fear responses (Bray et al., 2017). The integration of diverse auditory and olfactory stimuli is particularly beneficial in enhancing neural development. Such exposure promotes the formation of robust neural networks that underpin learning and memory, thereby conferring an adaptive advantage when confronted with novel situations later in life (Bray et al., 2017). By deliberately incorporating varied sensory experiences during this critical stage, breeders and caregivers can significantly bolster a puppy's capacity to cope with the complexities of its future environment.

The Importance of Early Handling by Humans

Human interaction during early development is a major determinant of a dog's subsequent behavioural profile. Early handling encompasses gentle, positive physical contact, verbal communication, and interactive play, all of which serve to familiarise puppies with human presence and reduce the risk of later fear or apprehension. Studies have consistently demonstrated that puppies receiving regular, positive handling exhibit reduced fearfulness and increased sociability in adulthood (Hiby et al., 2004). The tactile stimulation and calm verbal cues provided during early interactions help to shape the developing neural circuitry associated with stress regulation, leading to more resilient behavioural responses when faced with challenging situations (Riemer, 2015).

The method and frequency of handling are critical factors influencing these outcomes. Structured handling protocols that gradually introduce puppies to varied forms of human contact have been linked to the establishment of secure attachments and a positive perception of human interaction. Such protocols typically involve systematic sessions that combine gentle touch with encouraging vocal interactions, thereby reinforcing positive behavioural patterns (Hiby et al., 2004; Riemer, 2015).

Moreover, early handling is not solely about immediate behavioural adjustment; it also has enduring neurobiological implications. The consistent, positive interactions experienced during the early learning window are associated with long-term alterations in neural pathways that govern emotional regulation and stress responsiveness. This neurobiological reorganisation contributes to a lower propensity for anxiety and behavioural disorders in later life. In contrast, puppies that experience minimal or adverse handling may be predisposed to heightened reactivity and difficulties in forming trusting relationships with humans (Riemer, 2015).

The cumulative benefits of early human handling are evident in the adult dog's ability to integrate into multifaceted social settings with both humans and other dogs. By fostering a secure, positive association with human contact during the sensitive developmental period, early handling practices contribute to the overall welfare and functionality of the animal.

Chapter Highlights

- The critical socialisation window, approximately spanning three to fourteen weeks of age, is essential for the acquisition of foundational social skills and emotional regulation.

- Maternal care not only provides vital physical nourishment but also imparts behavioural guidance that underpins secure attachment and effective stress management.

- Littermate play and interaction are crucial for learning social communication, conflict resolution, and the establishment of behavioural norms that promote long-term social competence.

- Early, positive handling by humans is instrumental in reducing fearfulness, enhancing stress regulation, and establishing a secure, trusting relationship that supports lifelong behavioural health.

CHAPTER 5
SENSORY DEVELOPMENT

Puppies have an underdeveloped sensory system in the initial phase after their birth. The sensory development continues during the postnatal period. For the first two weeks, puppies are unable to see the world they are born into as their eyes do not open when they are around the age of 14 to 21 days old. This limited sensory development makes it challenging for them to interact with their surroundings.

Onset of Sensory Abilities

The subsequent opening of these sensory gateways marks the commencement of rapid neural and behavioural maturation.

1. **Visual Development**

The development of vision in puppies follows a precise temporal sequence. Typically, the eyelids begin to separate between 10 and 16 days after birth (King et al., 2016). This initial opening is a critical event; however, the acquisition of functional vision extends beyond mere exposure to light. During the early phase of visual experience, the retina undergoes significant maturation, and the visual cortex begins to process basic forms and motion. Studies indicate that although puppies initially perceive only high-contrast shapes, their ability to discern finer details and colours improves over subsequent weeks (Mills, 2013).

The progression from rudimentary light perception to refined visual processing is underpinned by synaptic plasticity within the visual cortex. Experience-dependent mechanisms, similar to those described in other mammals, facilitate the establishment of neural pathways essential for depth perception and spatial recognition (Katz and Shatz, 1996). This period of rapid visual development is not only pivotal for immediate survival—by enabling the detection of movement and potential threats—but also lays the foundation for more complex behaviours, including social communication and environmental exploration.

2. **Auditory Development**

Parallel to visual maturation, auditory development in puppies also follows a well-defined schedule. Although the anatomical structures necessary for hearing are present at birth, the ear canals remain closed until approximately 17 to 21 days of age (Jones and Peters, 2014). Once these canals open, puppies begin to respond to auditory stimuli, initially reacting to high-intensity sounds before gradually discriminating between different frequencies and sound patterns.

The emergence of auditory sensitivity is critical for the recognition of maternal calls and littermate vocalisations, which are integral to early social bonding and communication. As the auditory cortex matures, neural circuits become increasingly specialised, facilitating the discrimination of subtle auditory cues that may signal danger, food sources, or social opportunities (Jones and Peters, 2014). The refinement of hearing during this period is largely driven by environmental exposure; consistent interaction with a diverse range of sounds reinforces synaptic connectivity and improves auditory processing efficiency.

3. **Motor Coordination**

The development of motor coordination in puppies is closely linked to the maturation of their sensory systems. With the gradual acquisition of sight and hearing, puppies begin to explore their environment through increased mobility. Early motor skills are characterised by unsteady movements and basic reflex actions, but as sensory input is integrated, coordinated actions emerge. Research shows that by the third to fourth week of life, puppies exhibit enhanced control over their limbs, leading to improved balance and more purposeful locomotion (Brown and Smith, 2012).

This advancement in motor coordination is a product of both intrinsic neural maturation and extrinsic sensory stimulation. The cerebellum, responsible for the fine-tuning of motor activity, rapidly develops in conjunction with sensory areas of the brain. The interplay between sensory experiences and motor output allows puppies to adjust their movements in response to environmental feedback, thereby refining their ability to navigate complex settings (Brown and Smith, 2012). As neural circuits solidify, the efficiency of sensorimotor integration increases, which is essential for tasks such as playing, hunting, and later, executing more sophisticated behaviours.

Sensory Experiences and Brain Development

The initial acquisition of sensory abilities is only the beginning of a more complex process: the shaping of the brain through sensory experiences. During the early weeks of life, the brain exhibits a remarkable degree of plasticity, allowing it to adapt to environmental inputs and optimise neural pathways for future functionality.

1. **Neural Plasticity and Experience-Dependent Refinement**

Experience-dependent plasticity is a central concept in the development of sensory systems. As puppies are exposed to varied visual and auditory stimuli, their brains undergo structural and functional changes. Synaptic pruning and the strengthening of specific neural connections ensure that circuits become tailored to the statistical regularities of the environment (Martin and Lee, 2018). This process is especially prominent in the sensory cortices, where early exposure to diverse stimuli enhances the precision of neural responses.

Experimental evidence from studies on canids demonstrates that enriched sensory environments lead to more robust neural connectivity and improved cognitive function later in life (Almeida and Santos, 2018). In contrast, sensory deprivation or limited exposure during critical periods can result in lasting deficits in perceptual abilities. The dynamic interplay between sensory input and neural adaptation underscores the importance of early environmental diversity, not only for immediate sensory perception but also for the long-term optimisation of brain function.

2. **Multisensory Integration**

Another key aspect of sensory development is the integration of information across different modalities. The convergence of visual, auditory, and proprioceptive signals allows puppies to form a coherent representation of their surroundings. This multisensory integration occurs in specialised brain regions, where inputs from various senses are synthesised to guide behaviour and learning (Martin and Lee, 2018).

The process of multisensory integration enhances the efficiency of environmental navigation and the execution of coordinated motor responses. For instance, the simultaneous processing of sound and movement can alert a puppy to approaching stimuli, prompting timely behavioural responses. The neural mechanisms underlying this integration are highly adaptable, with experience fine-tuning the interactions between sensory modalities. The refinement of these processes is critical for the development of complex behaviours, including social interactions and problem-solving.

3. Long-Term Implications of Early Sensory Experiences

The formative influence of early sensory experiences extends well beyond the initial stages of development. The neural architecture established during this period has enduring effects on cognitive abilities and behavioural flexibility. Early exposure to a variety of sensory stimuli not only sharpens perceptual skills but also influences emotional regulation and stress responses.

Research indicates that puppies raised in environments that provide rich sensory stimulation tend to exhibit enhanced problem-solving abilities and a lower propensity for anxiety in later life (Mills, 2013). This relationship is attributed to the stable neural networks formed during the early critical period, which support adaptive responses to future challenges. Moreover, the integration of sensory and motor information during early development facilitates lifelong learning, as neural circuits remain responsive to new experiences while retaining the benefits of early optimisation.

The interdependence between sensory input and brain development suggests that interventions during the early postnatal period can have profound effects on the overall trajectory of canine cognitive and behavioural development. Ensuring that puppies are exposed to a broad range of sensory experiences is therefore critical not only for immediate perceptual acuity but also for the long-term functional organisation of the brain.

Chapter Highlights

- Puppies begin to gain functional vision between 10 and 16 days after birth, with hearing emerging around 17 to 21 days, and coordinated movement developing by the third to fourth week.

- The refinement of sensory systems is driven by experience-dependent plasticity, where diverse environmental stimuli enhance synaptic connectivity and perceptual accuracy.

- The integration of visual, auditory, and proprioceptive information is essential for forming a coherent understanding of the environment, thereby facilitating adaptive motor responses and complex behavioural patterns.

- Early sensory experiences have enduring effects on brain architecture, influencing cognitive abilities, emotional regulation, and behavioural flexibility throughout the lifespan.

CHAPTER 6
PLAY AND LEARNING

Puppies tend to learn a lot in the early weeks of their development when they still need their mom and littermates. From the age of 3 weeks, they start playing with their fellow puppies. The play is crucial to a puppy's development as they need to learn to be dogs. Though there is a lot we do not yet understand about play, it's widely accepted that play is an integral part of learning, including both social and motor skills.

The Science of Puppy Play

Puppies naturally engage in various forms of play from a young age, a phenomenon that is both biologically predetermined and environmentally influenced. The expression of playful behaviour is evident in activities ranging from vigorous physical interactions to more measured games of chase or tug-of-war. Such play is vital for refining motor skills and establishing a foundation for later social interactions.

1. **Physical Development**

The physical demands of play contribute significantly to the development of motor coordination and strength. Through activities such as chasing, tumbling, and wrestling, puppies enhance muscle tone and fine-tune their balance and agility. These actions promote not only skeletal and muscular growth but also stimulate the neural circuits responsible for motor planning and execution. Research has demonstrated that the vigorous physical exertion associated with play accelerates the maturation of the cerebellum, a brain region critical for coordinating movement (Burghardt, 2005). This accelerated development is instrumental in enabling puppies to respond to dynamic environments and execute co-ordinated actions that are essential for both survival and future learning.

Furthermore, the practice of varied motor skills during play provides a natural context for sensorimotor integration. The challenges encountered in play, such as adjusting to rapidly changing movement patterns, require the puppy to process sensory information efficiently and translate it into precise motor actions. This process, which involves rapid feedback and adaptation, is fundamental to the development of refined motor control. The cumulative effect of these experiences is a robust physical foundation that supports not only immediate play but also more complex behaviours later in life.

2. Social Development

In addition to fostering physical maturation, play serves as a critical medium for social learning. Interactions with littermates and other dogs during play offer puppies the opportunity to acquire and practise social skills that will govern their interactions throughout life. These playful encounters provide a structured context in which puppies learn to interpret communicative signals, negotiate roles, and establish behavioural boundaries. For example, during play, puppies practise bite inhibition—a skill essential for preventing injuries during interactions—and learn to modulate their intensity based on the responses of their playmates. Such experiences lay the groundwork for understanding social hierarchies and building cooperative relationships (Pellis and Pellis, 2009).

Social play is characterised by its spontaneous and self-moderating nature. Unlike directed training sessions, play allows puppies to experiment with different social strategies without the immediate pressure of obtaining a specific outcome. This freedom supports the development of emotional intelligence and self-regulation, as puppies learn to manage excitement and frustration in a safe context. The interplay between playful aggression and gentle contact during these interactions is a natural mechanism through which social bonds are reinforced, and individual temperaments are shaped. The observational learning that occurs during these sessions is critical, as puppies often mimic the behaviours of more experienced peers, thereby accelerating their own social competence.

3. Curiosity, Problem-Solving, and Confidence Building

Curiosity drives puppies to explore their surroundings, an instinctive behaviour that is integrally linked to the acquisition of problem-solving skills. This exploratory behaviour is not random; it is directed by an inherent motivation to discover, understand, and interact with novel stimuli. Such encounters stimulate cognitive processes that underpin learning and memory, reinforcing neural connections in regions associated with executive function and decision-making.

Engaging in play that involves problem-solving, such as navigating obstacles or manipulating objects to retrieve a reward, challenges puppies to employ strategies and adapt to unexpected outcomes. These activities enhance neural plasticity by encouraging the development of new synaptic connections and the refinement of existing ones. Engagement with novel challenges during play stimulates the prefrontal cortex, which is responsible for planning, attention, and inhibitory control. As puppies solve problems during play, they gain a sense of mastery over their environment, which in turn fosters self-assurance and resilience when confronted with unfamiliar situations (Kaminski and Marshall-Pescini, 2014).

When puppies successfully overcome challenges, the resultant positive feedback reinforces exploratory behaviour and increases their willingness to engage with complex tasks in the future. This cycle of exploration, challenge, and achievement contributes to a robust cognitive framework that supports lifelong learning. In environments that present varied and unpredictable stimuli, the ability to navigate and solve problems is a crucial determinant of future success. By honing these skills early on, puppies build a reservoir of adaptive strategies that underpin confident decision-making throughout their lives.

Moreover, the experience of overcoming obstacles during play has been shown to mitigate stress and reduce anxiety. Positive outcomes in problem-solving scenarios trigger the release of neurotransmitters such as dopamine, which not only enhance mood but also promote further exploratory behaviours. This neurochemical reinforcement creates a feedback loop in which curiosity and problem-solving are continually linked to feelings of reward and accomplishment. Consequently, puppies that engage in regular, diverse play are better equipped to handle stress and are less likely to develop maladaptive behaviours in response to future challenges.

Chapter Highlights

- Puppy play is essential for enhancing motor coordination and stimulating neural circuits responsible for sensorimotor integration, thereby establishing a strong physical and cognitive foundation.

- Playful interactions enable puppies to learn critical social skills, such as bite inhibition and communication, which are vital for forming positive relationships and navigating social hierarchies.

- Engaging in problem-solving during play not only reinforces neural plasticity but also fosters exploratory behaviour that underpins effective decision-making and adaptability.

- The challenges encountered and overcome during play contribute to a positive feedback loop, enhancing confidence and reducing the likelihood of anxiety by linking successful problem-solving with rewarding neurochemical responses.

CHAPTER 7

BRAIN DEVELOPMENT AND EMOTIONS

As puppies are growing physically, they simultaneously undergo emotional development. During the initial 12 months, they interact with their environment and learn what they like, what they are afraid of and what keeps them safe. Moreover, they also learn who to love and adore. By learning about the emotional development of the puppy, guardians can prepare a healthy and loving life for the puppy.

Brain Development and Emotional Regulation

1. Brain Development

From birth, puppies experience accelerated neural proliferation, synaptogenesis, and myelination that collectively establish the foundation for future cognitive and emotional functions. Key brain regions include the prefrontal cortex, amygdala, and hippocampus which undergo substantial growth during the early postnatal period. These structures are instrumental in processing sensory information, forming memories, and managing emotional responses (Feng et al., 2014). The rapid establishment of synaptic connections occurs in tandem with the fine-tuning of inhibitory and excitatory pathways, ensuring that neural activity remains balanced and adaptive.

Activity-dependent plasticity plays a critical role during this period. As puppies interact with their surroundings, neural circuits are modified in response to specific stimuli. This plasticity enables the developing brain to adapt to environmental challenges and form the neural networks necessary for sophisticated emotional regulation. The maturation of neural circuits is highly sensitive to the quality and diversity of early experiences, meaning that the environment can have lasting effects on the structure and function of the brain.

2. Emotional Regulation

Emotional regulation in puppies is governed by an intricate network of brain regions and neurochemical systems. The amygdala, which is central to the detection and processing of emotionally salient stimuli, works in concert with the prefrontal cortex to modulate behavioural responses. As these regions mature, puppies gradually acquire the capacity to control impulsive actions and adapt their responses to stressors appropriately (McGowan et al., 2009). Neurotransmitters, particularly serotonin and dopamine, are pivotal in fine-tuning these regulatory processes by mediating mood and behavioural control.

Another essential component in emotional regulation is the hypothalamic-pituitary-adrenal (HPA) axis. This neuroendocrine system governs the secretion of cortisol, a hormone critical for managing stress. In puppies, early experiences can recalibrate the sensitivity of the HPA axis, thereby influencing how stress is perceived and managed later in life. Positive environmental exposures during critical developmental windows tend to promote a more resilient stress response, whereas negative experiences may heighten vulnerability to anxiety and emotional dysregulation. The adaptive modifications observed in the HPA axis are underpinned not only by structural changes in neural circuits but also by epigenetic mechanisms that adjust gene expression in response to environmental cues.

The Role of Genetics Versus Environment in Shaping Personality

The relative influence of genetics and environment in shaping personality has been a longstanding debate in behavioural science. In puppies, genetic factors provide the initial blueprint for brain development and behavioural predispositions. Specific gene variants have been linked to traits such as sociability, reactivity, and even predispositions to fear or aggression. Research has demonstrated that different breeds exhibit distinct personality profiles, indicating a significant hereditary component in behavioural tendencies (Serpell, 1996).

Nonetheless, genetic predispositions do not determine outcomes in isolation. Environmental factors range from early-life social interactions to exposure to varied stimuli play a crucial role in either reinforcing or modulating inherent tendencies. During the sensitive periods of neural development, environmental inputs can lead to epigenetic modifications: chemical alterations to DNA that affect gene expression without changing the genetic code itself (Davenport et al., 2019). These modifications may amplify or suppress genetically determined traits, thereby influencing the trajectory of emotional development and personality.

For instance, a puppy with an inherited predisposition toward heightened reactivity might develop robust coping mechanisms if raised in an environment that offers balanced and controlled challenges. Conversely, the absence of adequate environmental enrichment can exacerbate inherent vulnerabilities, leading to maladaptive emotional responses. Thus, while the genetic framework provides a range of potential behavioural outcomes, environmental experiences during early development largely determine which of these potentials is realised.

Chapter Highlights

- Puppies experience accelerated brain development postnatally, with essential regions such as the prefrontal cortex, amygdala, and hippocampus establishing the basis for emotional regulation.

- The coordinated activity of neural circuits and neurotransmitter systems, along with the adaptive functioning of the HPA axis, underpins effective management of stress and emotional responses.

- While genetic predispositions provide a blueprint for behavioural tendencies, early-life environmental experiences play a decisive role in realising or mitigating these traits.

- Understanding the integration of genetic and environmental influences on brain development offers opportunities for early interventions that promote emotional resilience and balanced personality development in puppies.

CHAPTER 8

COMMUNICATION AND BODY LANGUAGE

A dog guardian must understand and interpret the language of the puppy. Knowledge of the body language of the puppy helps identify what the little buddy is trying to tell. When the guardians do not understand the body language, they tend to misunderstand what the puppy is trying to say. For instance, when a puppy wags its tail, it is commonly understood to be a sign of a happy and friendly dog. It might be, but it can be something else as well.

How Puppies Express Themselves

1. Vocalisation

Vocal expressions in puppies serve as important indicators of internal emotional states and social needs. Research has shown that different vocalisations have distinct purposes. For example, whining is commonly observed when puppies are experiencing distress or seeking attention from their littermates or caregivers. Experimental studies have revealed that high-pitched whines are frequently emitted when puppies experience separation from their primary social group (Waller and Caeiro, 2013).

Barking, in contrast, can signal a range of emotions such as excitement, fear or territoriality. The acoustic properties of barks, including frequency and duration, have been found to correlate with specific emotional contexts. Studies indicate that puppies produce varying barking patterns when exposed to novel stimuli compared with familiar ones (Marshall-Pescini et al., 2018). These variations help members of the social group quickly assess the situation and respond accordingly.

Low-intensity growls and howls are also part of the vocal repertoire in puppies. Such sounds may function as warnings or gentle cautions during social interactions and play. The structure of these vocalisations often encodes information about the sender's size and strength. A careful analysis of vocal tone and pitch can thus provide observers with clues regarding the puppy's emotional state and intentions (Waller and Caeiro, 2013). Researchers emphasise the need to consider the context in which these vocalisations occur because similar sounds can have different meanings depending on the situation.

2. Body Posture

Body posture is a critical element of non-verbal communication and provides visual signals that often complement vocal expressions. A relaxed body, with a loosely held tail and soft eyes, generally indicates contentment and a state of calm. In contrast, a tense body with raised fur, a stiff tail and a fixed gaze typically suggests fear or aggression.

Tail movement is a prominent feature in canine body language, yet its meaning is not always straightforward. Studies have demonstrated that the speed and direction of tail wagging can indicate different emotional states. For instance, a slow wag accompanied by a low tail may reflect insecurity, whereas a rapid, wide wag with the tail held high is associated with excitement and confidence (Hall and Carter, 2016).

Ear positioning also provides important cues. When a puppy holds its ears forward, it is often a sign of alertness and interest. Conversely, ears that are held flat against the head may suggest fear or submission. Additional factors such as head orientation and overall body alignment further refine the interpretation of a puppy's emotional state. Scientific investigations have documented that puppies adjust their posture responsively when interacting with both conspecifics and humans, thereby facilitating effective communication (Hall and Carter, 2016).

Facial expressions, although subtle in young dogs, can reveal much about a puppy's feelings. Minor changes in the position of the eyes and mouth have been associated with expressions of happiness, distress or anticipation. When combined with other postural cues, these facial signals offer a comprehensive picture of a puppy's emotional state. Research in this area has highlighted that the integration of multiple non-verbal signals improves the accuracy of emotion recognition in canine communication (Hall and Carter, 2016).

3. **Play Signals**

Play is an essential aspect of a puppy's development and an important arena for communication. During play, puppies employ a distinct set of signals to ensure that their interactions are interpreted as friendly rather than aggressive. One of the most recognisable signals is the play bow. In this gesture, the puppy lowers its front part while keeping the hindquarters elevated. This clear visual signal communicates an invitation to play and is understood by both dogs and humans.

Exaggerated and rhythmic movements also play a crucial role in playful communication. Behaviours such as bouncing, rolling over and chasing are performed in a manner that emphasises a non-threatening intent. Empirical studies have found that puppies who frequently engage in play exhibit higher levels of social synchronisation and coordination when interacting with their peers (Marshall-Pescini et al., 2018).

In addition to these signals, puppies often employ gentle mouthing and the deliberate extension of a paw during play. These behaviours serve to negotiate the rules of engagement and to signal submission when necessary. Research has demonstrated that puppies who use a broad range of play signals develop superior social skills and are more adept at resolving conflicts in later stages of life (Waller and Caeiro, 2013). The complexity and diversity of play signals underscore their role in facilitating social bonding and learning appropriate interaction protocols.

4. Interpreting Puppy Communication

For caregivers, the ability to interpret a puppy's communication accurately is essential to meet its needs effectively and to foster a secure bond. By integrating vocal, postural and play signals, one can gain a holistic understanding of the puppy's current emotional state and intentions. For example, a puppy that barks while simultaneously displaying a relaxed posture and gentle tail wagging is likely expressing excitement or seeking interaction. In contrast, barking paired with a tense body and flattened ears may indicate distress or fear.

Researchers advise that no single behavioural indicator should be considered in isolation. A combination of signals observed over time is the most reliable method for assessing a puppy's mood. Caregivers who are attentive to these subtle cues are better positioned to adjust their responses accordingly. For instance, if a puppy shows signs of stress through a combination of high-pitched vocalisations and a rigid posture, modifying the environment or providing comfort can prevent the escalation of anxiety (Hall and Carter, 2016).

Early and consistent exposure to positive human interaction has also been shown to enhance the clarity of a puppy's communication signals. Studies indicate that puppies raised with responsive caregiving are more effective at conveying their needs and are more readily understood by their human companions (Marshall-Pescini et al., 2018). This reciprocal communication not only strengthens the bond between the puppy and the caregiver but also promotes the development of a balanced and confident adult dog.

Chapter Highlights

- Vocalisations in puppies convey a range of emotions from distress to excitement, with the acoustic properties of sounds providing important clues about the emotional context.

- Body posture, including tail wagging, ear positioning and facial expressions, offers clear visual signals that help in assessing a puppy's mood accurately.

- Play signals such as the play bow and rhythmic movements are essential for establishing a friendly context and contribute to the development of strong social skills.

- A comprehensive understanding of a puppy's communication enhances caregiver responsiveness, strengthening the bond and promoting balanced emotional and social development.

CHAPTER 9

THE ROLE OF AROUSAL AND STRESS

Stress and arousal have a mind-altering effect on the development of dogs into adulthood. When puppies are exposed to stressful situations, they tend to display certain behaviours. If these behaviours are interpreted wrongly by the caregiver, it can negatively affect the puppy. A moderate level of stress or arousal is bearable for the puppy and helps in the positive development of attention, memory and retention. However, if puppies are exposed to high levels of stress and arousal, it can negatively affect them. Therefore, dog guardians need to learn when the puppy is stressed or aroused.

Puppies Response to Arousal and Stress

Puppies exhibit distinct physiological changes when confronted with stress. Activation of the hypothalamic-pituitary-adrenal axis results in elevated cortisol levels and increased heart rate (Beerda et al., 1998). Such responses prepare the animal for immediate action and have an adaptive value in novel or challenging situations. These measurable changes provide a scientific basis for recognising and interpreting stress in young canines. Behaviourally, puppies under stress may show signs of avoidance, increased alertness or subtle displacement activities. Observations include trembling, lip licking and yawning. These specific indicators provide practical cues for trainers to assess the emotional state of a puppy (Beerda et al., 1998). Accurate identification of these behaviours allows for timely intervention during training sessions.

Arousal plays a critical role in learning. Research demonstrates that moderate levels of arousal support attention and memory, whereas excessive stress impairs cognitive performance (Casey et al., 2014). The relationship between arousal and performance follows an inverted U-shaped curve, a phenomenon widely recognised in psychology. Puppies that experience overwhelming arousal may find it difficult to focus on new tasks, thereby hindering the acquisition of desired behaviours. Conversely, insufficient arousal may result in low engagement, limiting the effectiveness of the training session. Trainers must therefore design sessions that maintain an optimal level of stimulation.

Training approaches that promote moderate arousal lead to better outcomes. Short, focused sessions minimise the duration of stress exposure and prevent cognitive overload. Puppies benefit from learning in environments where stimuli are introduced gradually. Controlled exposure to novel experiences helps to build resilience and supports long-term behavioural development (Casey et al., 2014). This evidence supports the inclusion of varied yet predictable elements in training protocols.

Practical Tips for Managing Overstimulation

Practical strategies for managing overstimulation during training are essential. Scheduling sessions at times, when puppies are naturally calm, can reduce background stress. A consistent routine limits uncertainty and fosters a sense of security. Allocating a quiet area where puppies can withdraw when necessary, further supports emotional stability.

Gradual desensitisation is an effective method for reducing overstimulation. Introducing a low-intensity version of a stimulus and incrementally increasing its intensity allows puppies to acclimate without provoking a marked stress response. Empirical studies have demonstrated that controlled exposure contributes to more robust coping mechanisms (Mendl et al., 2010). This method requires close observation of the puppy's reactions so that the progression of stimulus intensity is tailored to the individual. Positive reinforcement techniques offer additional benefits by associating challenging situations with rewarding outcomes. Reward-based training helps to mitigate stress and reinforces the desired behaviour simultaneously. Delivering rewards immediately after the correct behaviour enhances the learning process and helps to establish a positive emotional context.

Environmental management also plays a significant role in minimising stress. Reducing unexpected noises and abrupt movements in the training area lowers the risk of overstimulation. Organising the space to limit distractions enables puppies to concentrate on the training tasks at hand. Research indicates that such controlled settings improve focus and facilitate the absorption of new information (Casey et al., 2014). Moreover, individual differences must be considered when implementing training strategies. Variations in temperament and early experiences influence how puppies respond to stress and arousal. Assessing each puppy's baseline stress levels in controlled conditions can offer valuable guidance in designing tailored training protocols. An individualised approach ensures that each puppy receives the level of support required for optimal learning.

Incorporating rest intervals within training sessions further contributes to effective stress management. Brief periods of calm allow puppies to recover from the demands of training. Activities that encourage relaxation during breaks have been shown to restore a puppy's readiness to learn. Such practices help to prevent the accumulation of stress over multiple sessions (Mendl et al., 2010).

The cumulative effects of early-life stress emphasise the importance of preventive measures. Prolonged or repeated high arousal during critical developmental stages may result in lasting behavioural challenges. Reducing exposure to excessive stress not only improves immediate training outcomes but also supports long-term emotional regulation and overall welfare. The integration of scientific insights into the design of training programmes offers a robust framework for managing arousal and stress in puppies. Evidence-based strategies that include controlled exposure, positive reinforcement and environmental adjustments contribute to a balanced learning experience. By addressing the individual needs of each puppy and providing appropriate rest, trainers can promote effective learning while protecting animal welfare.

Chapter Highlights

- Monitoring physiological and behavioural indicators is essential for identifying stress and adjusting training methods promptly.

- Maintaining an optimal level of arousal through controlled exposure, positive reinforcement and structured routines enhances cognitive performance and learning.

- Customised training strategies and rest intervals are critical in preventing chronic stress and ensuring long-term emotional well-being.

CHAPTER 10
COMMON PUPPY BEHAVIOURS

Puppies naturally display behaviours such as nipping, chewing and jumping during their early development. Each of these actions has a specific origin and function in the context of canine growth. Scientific investigation into these behaviours provides valuable insights into their underlying causes and offers guidance for guardians and trainers on how to shape them into appropriate conduct.

Nipping

Nipping is a prevalent form of communication during play among puppies. It serves as a mechanism for learning bite inhibition and establishing social boundaries. When littermates interact, a measured level of biting conveys feedback regarding the acceptable force of play. Research indicates that such interactions are vital for social development and for preventing future aggressive tendencies (Hiby et al., 2004). However, when nipping is directed towards humans, it is important to intervene early. Gentle redirection to an acceptable alternative, such as a chew toy, can help puppies learn that mouthing people is not permitted. This targeted approach reduces the likelihood that nipping will develop into an unwanted behaviour in later life.

Chewing

Chewing is an innate exploratory behaviour that assumes additional importance during the teething period. Oral exploration enables puppies to gather information about the world around them. At the same time, the discomfort associated with teething motivates puppies to seek relief through persistent mouthing of available objects. Studies confirm that the provision of suitable chew toys effectively channels this instinct. Appropriate objects for chewing not only alleviate the pain associated with teething but also contribute to the development of healthy oral motor skills (Hiby et al., 2004). In environments where no acceptable alternatives are available, puppies may resort to destructive chewing on household items. Early intervention with a variety of engaging chew options is therefore essential to foster beneficial oral habits.

Jumping

Jumping is a frequent response to excitement and social interaction in puppies. When meeting people or other animals, puppies often express enthusiasm by leaping upwards. This behaviour, although instinctive, may be misinterpreted as over-exuberance in a domestic setting. Research has demonstrated that jumping is more common in puppies that have not yet learned to regulate their arousal levels (Casey et al., 2014). The corrective approach for jumping focuses on teaching alternative forms of greeting. By withholding attention until the puppy's demeanour is calm, trainers reinforce the idea that composed behaviour is more rewarding than exuberant leaping. Consistent application of this strategy can result in a significant reduction in unwanted jumping over time.

Guiding Puppies to Better Behaviours

Effective management of nipping, chewing and jumping relies on strategies derived from an understanding of their natural motivations. Positive reinforcement stands out as a well-supported technique to shape behaviour. When a puppy exhibits controlled play or calm excitement, immediate rewards such as praise or treats solidify the connection between the behaviour and a positive outcome (Hiby et al., 2004). For instance, if a puppy resorts to nipping during play, the appropriate response is to redirect its attention to a toy. This direct substitution teaches the puppy that toys, rather than human hands, are acceptable outlets for biting impulses.

In the case of chewing, creating an environment rich in acceptable objects is imperative. Offering a range of textures and sizes in chew toys not only soothes teething discomfort but also satisfies the puppy's intrinsic desire to explore. Maintaining a consistent supply of appropriate chews reduces the temptation to seek out inappropriate items. Research shows that puppies provided with environmental enrichment experience fewer instances of destructive chewing (Serpell and Hsu, 2005). The success of this approach is contingent on the guardian's readiness to monitor and adjust the range of available options as the puppy grows.

Managing jumping centres on the regulation of excitement. The adoption of a no-reward policy when a puppy jumps ensures that the behaviour is not inadvertently reinforced. Guardians are encouraged to ignore the puppy until it has settled and then to reward calm behaviour with attention. This method effectively communicates that jumping does not yield the desired result. The gradual transition to alternative greeting behaviours is most successful when applied consistently in a variety of social contexts (Casey et al., 2014). In addition, time-outs may occasionally be employed as a brief period of isolation when excessive jumping persists. Such measures help the puppy to understand that overly excited behaviour results in a temporary loss of social interaction.

Another essential element in guiding these behaviours is the structured nature of the training environment. A routine that incorporates regular play and training sessions offers puppies a stable context in which to learn. The deliberate scheduling of activities reduces the risk of overstimulation, which can exacerbate nipping and jumping. Integrating socialisation sessions into the training programme further enables puppies to gain experience in interpreting social cues. Scientific evidence underlines that early socialisation has long-lasting effects on a puppy's behavioural responses (Serpell and Hsu, 2005). This approach not only addresses the immediate challenges posed by nipping, chewing and jumping but also lays the foundation for well-adjusted behaviour in adulthood.

Guardians and trainers should monitor each puppy's progress and adjust their methods according to individual needs. The variation in personality and sensitivity among puppies necessitates a flexible and observant approach. Tailored interventions based on careful observation led to more rapid and enduring behavioural improvements. The convergence of behavioural science and practical training techniques offers a reliable framework that benefits both the puppy and its guardian.

Chapter Highlights

- Early redirection of nipping towards acceptable alternatives is essential to foster proper social communication.

- Providing a variety of chew toys during the teething phase channels natural oral exploration and reduces destructive behaviour.

- Consistent training routines and positive reinforcement enable puppies to manage excitement, thereby reducing unwanted jumping.

CHAPTER 11

THE SCIENCE OF SOCIALISATION

The early experiences of the puppy shape how he perceives the world growing up. For instance, if the puppy has had traumatic experiences in his developmental phase, it may have a deep behavioural and psychological impact on the grown-up dog. During this sensitive phase of development, puppies are exposed to various stimuli and their interaction with people, dogs and the surrounding environment influences their emotional and social competence. According to scientific research, the quality and range of the experiences that a puppy has in the early phase shape his behavioural aspects and determine how well-adjusted the adult dog becomes.

Exposing Puppies to the World

The socialisation period generally occurs between three and fourteen weeks of age. Research has shown that puppies receiving varied and positive experiences during this interval develop reduced fear responses and increased adaptability later in life (Freedman et al., 1961). Controlled exposure to different stimuli allows the young animal to form associations that influence neural pathways and behavioural responses. During this phase, the brain is especially receptive to learning social cues and building adaptive responses.

Interactions with people play a central role in early socialisation. Regular, gentle encounters with individuals from various age groups and cultural backgrounds enable puppies to learn diverse communication signals. Such experiences help the animal develop trust and reduce the likelihood of anxiety when encountering unfamiliar people. Equally important is exposure to other animals. Meetings with conspecifics and representatives of other species provide puppies with the chance to observe and learn species-specific social skills. These interactions support a balanced understanding of social exchanges and reduce the risk of developing fear-based or aggressive responses.

Exposure to a variety of environments also contributes to positive developmental outcomes. Introducing puppies to different settings such as quiet parks, busy urban areas and calm indoor spaces enables them to learn how to interpret and cope with novel stimuli. These experiences encourage adaptability and lower the probability of stress when confronted with unfamiliar situations. Scientific studies indicate that early encounters with diverse surroundings help to build resilience by moderating neural responses to potential stressors (Wilson and Davison, 2006).

Long-Term Effects of Socialisation

The neurobiological basis of early socialisation is well documented. During the sensitive period, the brain undergoes significant development and exposure to varied social stimuli influences synaptic connections in regions associated with fear and social behaviour. This controlled stimulation leads to neural adaptations that support reduced stress reactivity in adult dogs. Research confirms that puppies with enriched social experiences display calmer responses and improved coping strategies when faced with challenging circumstances (Wilson and Davison, 2006). Long-term outcomes of comprehensive early socialisation are evident in adult behaviour. Dogs that have experienced a range of positive interactions tend to exhibit higher confidence when encountering novel situations. Empirical evidence reveals that early socialisation reduces the occurrence of behavioural problems such as excessive fear and anxiety. A well-socialised dog is better equipped to manage unpredictable or stressful situations. Findings from several studies suggest that early positive experiences lead to improved social competence and overall behavioural stability in later life (Valsecchi et al., 2010).

Implementing effective socialisation programmes requires careful planning and attention to the individual needs of each puppy. Structured sessions should include gradual exposure to people, animals and different settings while ensuring that the intensity of the stimuli is appropriate. Overwhelming a puppy with excessive stimulation may lead to adverse effects, whereas consistent and measured experiences promote the development of adaptive coping mechanisms. Scientific recommendations endorse a gradual and positive approach to exposure so that each new experience is processed within a supportive context.

The role of the caregiver is crucial during the socialisation process. Guardians and trainers must create a series of positive experiences that encourage curiosity and build trust. Gentle introductions and consistent routines help prevent the development of fear or avoidance behaviours. It is essential that early interactions are constructive and that any potentially stressful encounters are managed carefully. The lasting impact of early social experiences reinforces the importance of providing a nurturing and varied environment during the sensitive period.

Inadequate social exposure may result in a range of behavioural issues. Puppies with limited opportunities for socialisation can develop persistent fear responses and may struggle to adapt to new situations. Such difficulties can manifest as anxiety or aggressive behaviours in adulthood.

Research confirms that early social deficits are associated with challenges in adapting to unfamiliar circumstances and forming positive relationships with both humans and other animals (Freedman et al., 1961). Proactive socialisation measures are therefore an essential component of responsible dog guardianship.

When developing a socialisation plan, it is important to monitor each puppy's progress and adjust the approach as needed. Variations in personality and sensitivity among puppies necessitate flexibility and close observation. Tailored interventions based on individual reactions lead to more rapid and enduring behavioural improvements. The integration of behavioural science with practical training techniques offers a reliable framework that benefits both the puppy and its future interactions.

Early socialisation not only has immediate benefits but also influences the trajectory of a dog's emotional and social development throughout life. Positive early experiences have been linked to lower incidences of stress-related disorders and behavioural challenges in adulthood. Evidence indicates that a well-socialised dog is more likely to engage in appropriate interactions and display greater resilience in the face of environmental changes (Valsecchi et al., 2010). This long-term perspective underlines the importance of investing time and effort during the critical socialisation period.

By providing controlled, positive exposure to a variety of stimuli, caregivers can help puppies build a solid foundation for future confidence and well-being. Consistent application of these principles throughout early development supports the growth of a dog that is not only behaviourally stable but also capable of forming healthy and balanced relationships. The scientific evidence reinforces the view that early socialisation is a key determinant of lifelong behavioural outcomes, making it an essential consideration for every responsible dog guardian.

Chapter Highlights

- The critical socialisation period between three and fourteen weeks is essential for forming adaptive neural and behavioural responses.

- Gradual and controlled exposure to diverse stimuli, including people, animals and various environments, reduces the risk of fear-based behaviours.

- Positive and consistent social experiences during early development contribute to long-term confidence and improved coping strategies in adult dogs.

CHAPTER 12
POSITIVE TRAINING TECHNIQUES

Positive training techniques, commonly referred to as force-free training, are grounded in scientific principles of learning theory. This approach focuses on reinforcing desired behaviours rather than using punishment or coercion. By relying on rewards and consistent reinforcement, trainers enhance communication and build a strong bond with the dog. The method is supported by extensive research in behavioural psychology and neurobiology, which highlights its effectiveness and humane nature.

Scientific Basis of Force-Free Training

Behavioural psychology provides a robust framework for understanding why force-free training works best. Operant conditioning demonstrates that behaviours followed by rewarding outcomes are more likely to be repeated. In canine training, this means that when a desired behaviour is immediately reinforced, the associated neural pathways are strengthened (Hiby et al., 2004). Comparative studies have revealed that dogs trained with positive methods exhibit lower stress levels and greater confidence than those trained with aversive techniques (Blackwell et al., 2008). These results underscore the value of using a force-free approach to promote lasting behavioural change without inducing fear or anxiety.

1. Mechanisms of Reward and Reinforcement

The fundamental mechanism behind positive training lies in the effective use of rewards. When a dog performs a desired action, the immediate delivery of a treat, praise or play not only reinforces that behaviour but also stimulates the release of dopamine in the brain. This neurotransmitter plays a crucial role in pleasure and learning, which in turn promotes the repetition of the rewarded behaviour (Casey et al., 2014). The success of this method depends on the timing and consistency of the reinforcement. A reward must follow the behaviour closely enough to establish a clear and direct association, ensuring that the dog understands the cause-and-effect relationship. This precise application of reinforcement fosters a positive emotional state that is essential for effective learning.

2. Building Trust and Communication

The use of rewards and reinforcement in training serves a dual purpose: it facilitates learning and simultaneously builds trust between the dog and the trainer. A training environment that emphasises positive outcomes creates a secure space for the dog. Research has shown that dogs trained with reward-based techniques are more likely to engage willingly in training sessions, exhibit improved focus and respond better to commands (Hiby et al., 2004). This trust is a direct result of the absence of fear associated with punishment. Clear, consistent communication further strengthens this bond. When a dog recognises that specific actions lead to immediate and desirable rewards, it becomes more receptive to cues and demonstrates a greater willingness to cooperate. The resulting improvement in the dog's confidence and attentiveness forms the basis for a successful training programme.

Practical Applications of Positive Training Techniques

Implementing positive training techniques involves a systematic approach that ensures each session is effective and tailored to the dog's individual needs. The training environment should be free of distractions to allow the dog to focus on the task. A quiet and controlled setting enhances the learning process by minimising external stimuli that could otherwise divert the dog's attention.

Close observation of the dog's behaviour is essential to deliver rewards promptly. Recognising even subtle cues enables the trainer to reinforce the correct behaviour immediately, thereby solidifying the learning process. A varied selection of rewards, including treats, verbal praise and play, helps maintain the dog's motivation and prevents habituation. Research confirms that a diversity of reinforcers can sustain the dog's interest over extended training periods (Blackwell et al., 2008).

The use of clear and consistent cues is another critical element. Integrating verbal commands with gestures and body language improves the dog's ability to understand and respond to instructions. Multimodal communication has been shown to accelerate learning and improve the retention of new behaviours (Blackwell et al., 2008). Moreover, trainers are encouraged to adopt a personalised approach. Recognising that each dog has a unique temperament and pace of learning allows the training programme to be adjusted accordingly. This individualisation not only maximises the effectiveness of the training but also enhances the overall well-being of the dog by ensuring that it is not overwhelmed.

Force-free techniques are particularly effective when combined with ongoing monitoring and adaptation. Regular assessment of the dog's progress enables trainers to refine their approach, ensuring that reinforcement strategies remain effective as the dog develops. Scientific evidence supports the idea that a well-structured, reward-based training plan leads to more consistent behavioural outcomes and fosters a deeper bond between the dog and its guardian (Casey et al., 2014).

Chapter Highlights

- Science-based, force-free training methods utilise immediate and consistent rewards to reinforce desired behaviours, resulting in lower stress and enhanced learning.

- The release of dopamine during positive reinforcement creates a pleasurable learning experience that promotes behavioural repetition and long-term retention.

- Clear communication and personalised training approaches build trust between the dog and the trainer, leading to improved obedience and overall emotional well-being.

CHAPTER 13

BUILDING RESILIENCE

Building resilience in puppies is critical in the early period as it helps the dog recover from experiences of fear, frustration and anxiety. Resilience helps develop emotional stability and shape the puppy's behaviour over the course of his development. As per scientific research, early development plays an influential role in the transformation of neural circuits that regulate stress responses. When puppies have a well-developed resilience, it is easier for them to handle challenging situations and develop positive behavioural patterns.

Understanding Puppy Resilience

Resilience is not an innate trait but a skill that can be cultivated through structured experiences. Puppies are naturally exposed to novel stimuli that can induce mild fear or frustration. These responses activate physiological systems, including the hypothalamic-pituitary-adrenal axis, which in turn influence behavioural outcomes (Dreschel and Granger, 2009). The extent of recovery from such stressors is dependent on the intensity and duration of the exposure, as well as the environmental context. Early experiences that involve controlled and moderate stressors can prime puppies for better recovery in future challenging situations.

1. **Teaching Recovery from Fear and Frustration**

Effective strategies for teaching puppies to recover from fear and frustration centre on gradual exposure and positive reinforcement. Introducing puppies to manageable levels of stress allows them to learn that the experience is transient and controllable. For instance, exposing a puppy to a brief, non-threatening stimulus and then immediately providing a rewarding experience helps form a positive association. Over time, the puppy learns that recovery follows moments of fear. This approach involves recognising subtle signs of distress and intervening with a calm and reassuring presence. Consistent repetition of these controlled exposures aids in establishing a neural pathway that favours rapid recovery from negative emotional states.

2. **The Role of Consistency and Predictability**

Establishing a consistent routine is fundamental in reducing uncertainty, which can amplify fear and frustration. Predictability in daily interactions, feeding times, and play sessions fosters a sense of security in puppies. Regularity in the environment provides a framework within which puppies learn to anticipate outcomes, thereby diminishing the intensity of stress responses. Empirical evidence suggests that environments characterised by consistent patterns enable puppies to develop robust coping mechanisms (Freedman et al., 1961). By adhering to a predictable schedule, trainers and guardians communicate that the environment is stable, which reduces anxiety and reinforces the ability to recover from adverse experiences.

3. **Creating Safe Spaces**

Safe spaces are designated areas where puppies can retreat to recover from overstimulation or minor stressors. These environments are quiet, secure and free from excessive external stimuli. The availability of a safe space encourages self-soothing and provides an opportunity for the puppy to regulate its emotions. Research on stress recovery highlights that having a secure retreat can modulate physiological responses and lower the activation of stress hormones (Goddard and Beilharz, 1983). Safe spaces serve as a buffer during periods of high arousal and contribute to a more measured recovery process. In practice, a crate or a quiet room with familiar bedding can fulfil this role. The key is to ensure that the space is consistently available and associated with positive experiences rather than punishment or isolation.

Practical Applications in Puppy Development

Implementing strategies that foster resilience involves a combination of controlled exposure to mild stressors, establishing consistent routines and creating safe spaces. In practical terms, trainers and guardians should design environments that balance stimulation with recovery opportunities. During play or training sessions, introducing brief moments of frustration, such as delaying a reward for a few seconds can teach puppies that temporary discomfort leads to eventual positive outcomes. The emphasis must remain on clear communication and calm intervention to avoid overwhelming the puppy.

In addition, monitoring the puppy's behaviour closely enables timely adjustments to the level of challenge presented. The individual temperament of each puppy dictates the pace at which they adapt to stress. Customising the training regimen to suit the puppy's unique needs is essential. For some puppies, increased exposure to mildly challenging situations may be beneficial, whereas others may require extended periods in a safe space to recover fully. Over time, a balanced approach promotes not only resilience but also confidence, allowing the puppy to face new experiences with reduced anxiety.

A well-structured programme incorporates both environmental management and behavioural training. Consistency in cues, routines and responses creates a foundation upon which resilience is built. For instance, when a puppy displays signs of fear during a new experience, a calm voice and gentle touch can signal that the situation is manageable. Immediate access to a safe space, followed by a rewarding activity, reinforces the notion that recovery from fear is both expected and achievable. Such practices are supported by research showing that stable environments and predictable interactions contribute significantly to improved stress-coping abilities (Dreschel and Granger, 2009).

The gradual development of resilience in puppies has long-term implications for behavioural health. Resilient puppies are better prepared to face environmental challenges and are less likely to develop persistent anxiety or behavioural issues. The integration of controlled exposure, consistency and safe spaces creates a robust framework that supports both immediate recovery from negative experiences and overall emotional well-being. As these resilient behaviours become ingrained, the puppy is more likely to respond adaptively to stressors in adulthood, resulting in a more balanced and confident canine.

Chapter Highlights

- Controlled exposure to mild stressors, coupled with immediate positive reinforcement, teaches puppies to recover from fear and frustration effectively.

- Consistent routines and predictable environments reduce uncertainty and promote the development of strong coping mechanisms.

- Providing safe spaces enables puppies to regulate their emotions and recover from overstimulation, contributing to long-term emotional well-being.

CHAPTER 14

NUTRITION AND HEALTH

Optimal nutrition and early health care are critical factors in determining a puppy's physical development, cognitive capabilities, and behavioural outcomes. A balanced diet supplies the necessary energy and nutrients for rapid growth and supports brain development. Concurrently, timely vaccinations and regular veterinary examinations contribute to a strong immune system and overall health. Scientific research underpins the understanding of how diet and early healthcare interventions interact to influence the long-term well-being of dogs.

Impact of Diet on Growth

A balanced nutritional regimen is essential for supporting the rapid growth phase experienced by puppies. Diets formulated with appropriate levels of protein, fats, carbohydrates, vitamins, and minerals ensure that puppies receive the building blocks for healthy tissue development. Protein is particularly important for muscle formation, while calcium and phosphorus play key roles in skeletal development. Research has demonstrated that imbalances in these nutrients can result in stunted growth or developmental anomalies (Radcliffe et al., 2012). Nutritional deficiencies during early life may also predispose puppies to chronic health issues that affect their quality of life.

1. **Diet and Brain Development**

Brain development in puppies is highly dependent on the quality of their diet. Specific nutrients such as omega-3 fatty acids, particularly docosa-hexaenoic acid (DHA), are vital for the formation of neural tissues and synaptic connections. Antioxidants and certain vitamins contribute to reducing oxidative stress, thereby protecting developing brain cells. Studies have indicated that diets enriched with these nutrients are associated with improved cognitive performance and faster learning rates (Bauer et al., 2015). The composition of early diets can have lasting effects on neurological function, influencing memory, attention and problem-solving skills later in life.

2. **Diet and Behaviour**

The nutritional status of a puppy has implications that extend beyond physical growth. Behavioural patterns are influenced by the availability of essential nutrients, which modulate neurotransmitter synthesis and energy metabolism in the brain. A balanced diet may help mitigate behavioural issues by promoting stable energy levels and reducing irritability. Conversely, diets that lack proper nutrients have been linked to increased anxiety and reduced capacity for learning. Empirical evidence suggests that puppies receiving nutritionally balanced meals demonstrate improved social interactions and enhanced responsiveness during training sessions (Kraus et al., 2017). Thus, the diet not only supports physical and cognitive development but also contributes to emotional stability and adaptive behaviour.

3. **Vaccinations and Early Health Care**

Early health care practices, including vaccinations and routine veterinary check-ups, are fundamental in safeguarding the health of growing puppies. Vaccinations protect against infectious diseases that can compromise the immune system and impede development. Timely administration of vaccines helps to build immunity during the early stages of life when puppies are most vulnerable to infections. Research confirms that a structured vaccination programme significantly reduces the incidence of common canine diseases (Brown et al., 2018). Regular veterinary visits further facilitate the early detection and management of health issues, ensuring that any developmental concerns are addressed promptly.

4. The Role of Routine Veterinary Examinations

Routine veterinary examinations are integral to monitoring a puppy's progress and overall health. These visits provide an opportunity for veterinarians to assess nutritional status, growth patterns, and behavioural indicators of well-being. Early identification of potential health problems allows for swift intervention, which can prevent minor issues from escalating into serious conditions. In addition, regular health check-ups enable the adjustment of dietary plans based on the puppy's developmental stage and specific needs (Smith and Jones, 2016). Establishing a schedule of routine examinations contributes to the prevention of chronic diseases and supports a long-term healthy lifestyle.

Practical Applications in Nutrition and Health

The integration of a balanced diet with systematic early healthcare practices forms the foundation for robust canine development. Caregivers should select commercial diets or prepare home-cooked meals that meet the specific nutritional requirements of growing puppies. Special attention must be given to the inclusion of nutrients that support brain development and behavioural stability. Alongside proper feeding practices, adherence to vaccination schedules and routine veterinary examinations is essential. These measures ensure that puppies develop in a secure environment where physical growth, cognitive function, and emotional well-being are optimised. Regular communication between caregivers and veterinary professionals is crucial in adapting nutritional and healthcare strategies to meet the evolving needs of the puppy.

Chapter Highlights

- A balanced diet rich in proteins, essential fatty acids, and micronutrients is vital for proper physical growth, brain development, and stable behaviour in puppies.

- Early health care, including structured vaccination programmes and regular veterinary examinations, significantly contributes to disease prevention and early detection of developmental issues.

- Integrating sound nutritional practices with systematic early health care creates a robust foundation for long-term physical, cognitive, and emotional well-being in dogs.

CHAPTER 15
PUPPIES AND HUMAN WELL-BEING

When humans have puppies to take care of, it leads to physical and psychological benefits. As per scientific studies, when humans regularly interact with puppies, it leads to beneficial changes in human psychology and physiology which help improve mental health and contribute to a healthy relationship between the caregiver and the puppy. The relationship is based on trust, love and nurturing that leads to a positive impact on human life as well as contributes to the healthy development of the puppy.

Psychological Benefits of Living with Puppies

Puppies play an important role in alleviating stress and enhancing mood. Interaction with puppies has been shown to increase levels of oxytocin while reducing cortisol, which leads to lower stress and a more positive emotional state (Beetz et al., 2012). The playful nature of puppies encourages laughter and joy, thereby mitigating feelings of loneliness and depression. Engaging with a puppy stimulates social interactions that contribute to improved self-esteem and a sense of purpose. Scientific findings indicate that the neurochemical changes elicited by positive human-puppy interactions not only relieve acute stress but also build resilience against future psychological challenges.

1. Physical Benefits of Living with Puppies

Puppies promote physical health by encouraging active lifestyles. Routine activities, such as walking and playing, provide regular exercise that can improve cardiovascular health and reduce the risk of obesity. Research has shown that individuals who own puppies often experience lower blood pressure and improved heart rate variability compared to non-guardians (Odendaal and Meintjes, 2003). These physiological responses are directly related to the reduction in stress and anxiety associated with caring for a puppy. Additionally, the responsibilities of puppy care can foster increased mobility and social engagement, further supporting physical well-being. The cumulative effect of these benefits is reflected in enhanced overall fitness and reduced incidence of sedentary lifestyle-related health problems.

2. Enhancing Human-Animal Relationships Through Science

The science of human-puppy interactions provides a robust framework for understanding how mutual benefits are derived from these relationships. Neurobiological studies have demonstrated that interactions with puppies activate brain regions associated with reward and social bonding. These findings suggest that repeated engagement with puppies strengthens neural circuits involved in trust and empathy (Beetz et al., 2012). Scientific investigations into the behavioural responses of puppies have also informed training techniques that promote positive communication. Knowledge of canine behaviour and development allows guardians to interact in ways that are mutually beneficial, thus fostering a harmonious and respectful relationship. The integration of behavioural science into everyday practices ensures that the bond between humans and puppies is both emotionally enriching and sustainable over time.

3. **Practical Applications in Daily Life**

The benefits of puppy guardianship extend into daily routines, with practical applications that enhance human well-being. Scheduled outdoor walks and structured play sessions not only contribute to the puppy's socialisation and training but also serve as regular opportunities for physical exercise for the guardian. Research suggests that predictable, routine interactions reduce stress by providing a sense of order and security for both the puppy and the guardian (Friedmann and Son, 2009). In addition, engaging in activities such as grooming and interactive training sessions reinforces the bond between the puppy and its human companion. These practices are enhanced by an understanding of canine behaviour, enabling guardians to recognise and respond to subtle cues. Such responsiveness not only improves the puppy's behaviour but also cultivates patience and empathy in the guardian, key attributes that contribute to overall psychological health.

Moreover, the structured nature of positive interaction creates opportunities for broader social engagement. Participation in dog training classes, community dog-walking groups and social events cantered around puppies often leads to new social connections and reduced feelings of isolation. The communal aspect of puppy care has been linked to improved social support networks, which are critical for maintaining mental health. In this context, the science of human-puppy interactions is instrumental in developing programmes and interventions that integrate animal-assisted activities into public health strategies. Data from wearable technology further confirm that consistent interaction with puppies is associated with measurable improvements in cardiovascular and stress-related parameters. These objective findings underscore the value of integrating puppy-based activities into daily routines and community health initiatives.

When dog guardians know the scientific principles related to puppies' developmental phases, it positively impacts the relationship between the guardian and the growing puppy. According to research in neuroscience, developmental psychology, and behavioural science, a puppy's early experiences shape his cognitive, social, and emotional capabilities. For instance, studies have demonstrated that positive social interactions during critical developmental periods foster secure attachment and reliable behavioural patterns (Freedman et al., 1961). Such insights empower dog guardians and trainers to apply informed care practices that enhance learning and promote long-term resilience.

Scientific evidence further supports that a balanced approach incorporating consistent training, proper nutrition and regular health care is essential. Reward-based training methods, underpinned by operant conditioning principles, have been shown to reduce stress and reinforce desirable behaviours (Hiby et al., 2004). These methods strengthen the human-animal bond by building trust through positive communication and predictable routines. Concurrently, attention to nutritional needs and preventive health measures supports both physical growth and cognitive function. The integration of these elements establishes a robust foundation for lifelong health and stability in dogs.

The neurobiological benefits of nurturing puppy care extend beyond the animal itself. Interaction with puppies has been associated with increased oxytocin levels in humans, which enhances social bonding and emotional balance (Beetz et al., 2012). This biological response contributes to improved mood and reduced stress, making the experience of raising a puppy mutually rewarding. Moreover, consistent engagement in daily activities such as walks, play and training not only advances the dog's development but also encourages physical exercise and mental well-being in their human companions.

A science-based approach to puppy care calls for patience, informed decision-making and a commitment to continual learning. By recognising the importance of each developmental stage, caregivers can tailor their methods to meet the evolving needs of their growing dog. Proactive measures, such as adapting training techniques during adolescence and ensuring routine veterinary assessments, help maintain a harmonious progression from puppyhood to adulthood. Informed strategies based on empirical research enable guardians to address challenges effectively while reinforcing the bond that develops from shared positive experiences.

Ultimately, the wealth of scientific research available highlights the multifaceted benefits of understanding puppy development. Nurturing a puppy with care, patience and evidence-based practices yields lasting rewards in terms of behavioural stability, physical health and emotional fulfilment. The lifelong bond forged between dogs and their guardians is enhanced by applying these insights, resulting in a relationship characterised by mutual trust, joy and well-being.

Puppy Development Timeline

Puppy development follows a structured sequence that begins at birth and extends into adulthood. In the first two weeks, puppies depend entirely on their mother while their sensory systems are immature. From two to four weeks, their eyes open and initial reactions to sounds and smells occur. The period from four to eight weeks involves rapid physical growth, weaning and the early acquisition of social skills through interaction with littermates and caregivers. Between eight and twelve weeks, puppies enter a vital socialisation phase during which they learn basic commands and acceptable behaviour. From three to six months, the onset of adolescence is marked by increased independence and teething. Beyond six months, dogs begin to stabilise physically and behaviourally, although continued socialisation and training remain important for long-term adjustment.

Quick Tips for Common Puppy Challenges

Managing everyday puppy challenges requires clear and practical strategies. To address house training, set a regular schedule that offers frequent opportunities for outdoor relief. Observe the puppy closely and provide immediate positive feedback for successful elimination outside. When nipping occurs, gently interrupt the action and redirect the puppy to an appropriate chew toy. For issues with destructive chewing, ensure a selection of safe, engaging items is available to alleviate teething discomfort. Facilitate positive social interactions by organising controlled meetings with other dogs and people in calm settings. When a puppy experiences separation anxiety, introduce short intervals of alone time within a secure environment, gradually increasing the duration as the puppy adjusts. To manage high energy levels, incorporate brief training sessions that offer mental challenges and physical exercise. All techniques should be applied with patience and adapted to the individual temperament and stage of development, ensuring that the puppy learns to cope with common challenges effectively.

Chapter Highlights

- Interaction with puppies increases oxytocin and reduces cortisol, resulting in lower stress and improved mood.

- Regular physical activities associated with puppy care contribute to enhanced cardiovascular health and overall fitness.

- Applying scientific insights into human-puppy interactions fosters strong, positive relationships that benefit both individual well-being and broader community health.

CHAPTER 16
FROM PUPPY TO TEENAGER

As puppies mature, they transition through adolescence into adulthood, a period marked by significant physiological, hormonal, and behavioural changes. Scientific research indicates that this phase is crucial for the consolidation of early experiences and the refinement of learned skills. A structured approach that adapts to evolving developmental needs is essential for ensuring that a puppy grows into a happy, well-adjusted dog.

Preparing for Adolescence

Adolescence in dogs is characterised by increased independence, hormonal fluctuations, and evolving social dynamics. During this period, neural plasticity remains high, meaning that experiences continue to shape behavioural outcomes. The challenges encountered include heightened impulsiveness, testing of boundaries, and the potential emergence of undesirable behaviours if early interventions are not maintained. Structured socialisation sessions and consistent training methods play a key role in mitigating these issues. Controlled exposure to varied environments and novel stimuli reinforces self-regulation and builds adaptive coping mechanisms. Early intervention in this stage is critical; research shows that puppies who receive sustained, positive reinforcement during this sensitive period are more likely to develop stable behavioural patterns (Freedman et al., 1961).

At around 8-10 months old dogs start to become teenagers, and unsurprisingly adolescence is one of the most dynamic and challenging stages in a dog's life. It is a period of heightened energy, exploratory behaviour, and social sensitivity. Adolescence in dogs is a critical developmental period marked by significant physiological, behavioural, and hormonal changes. This stage typically occurs between six months and two years of age, depending on the breed and individual factors. It is a time when young dogs transition from juvenile dependence to adult independence.

During adolescence, dogs experience rapid physical growth and sexual maturation. Puberty starts with the production of sex hormones such as testosterone in males and oestrogen in females, which triggers profound changes in behaviour and physiology. Research shows that testosterone levels in male dogs peak during adolescence and affect their behaviours such as mounting, roaming, and increased aggression (Beach, 1974). Studies indicate that the prefrontal cortex which is responsible for decision-making and impulse control is still in the process of maturing during this period (Pang et al., 2021). Consequently, adolescent dogs may exhibit impulsivity and difficulty in adhering to learned behaviours, even when they are well-trained as puppies.

Behaviourally, adolescence is a time of exploration and risk-taking. Dogs may display increased curiosity, independence, and sensitivity to environmental stimuli. It is also the time of "adolescent regression," where previously learned cues or behaviours may appear to be forgotten. Such behavioural fluctuations are rooted in the ongoing maturation of neural pathways and hormonal influences (Feng et al., 2015).

Adolescent dogs test boundaries within their pack or human family socially. They tend to challenge authority figures, exhibit selective hearing, or engage in play that appears rougher or more competitive. These behaviours are natural expressions of a dog's developmental drive to assert individuality and determine their social rank (Udell and Wynne, 2010). The adolescent phase often tests the patience of dog guardians. Behavioural issues such as excessive chewing, digging, or barking can emerge during this time.

The Positive, Science-Based Approach

When it comes to canine training, methodologies have evolved significantly based on scientific discoveries and an improved understanding of animal behaviour. Central to this transformation is the shift toward positive, science-based approaches that emphasise evidence-backed practices while rejecting outdated dominance-based models.

- **Evidence-Based Practices**

Evidence-based practices in canine training draw from disciplines such as behavioural science, ethology, and psychology to develop humane and effective techniques. Research demonstrates that dogs, like other animals, learn optimally through reward-based systems, where desired behaviours are reinforced with positive stimuli. This approach aligns with operant conditioning principles proposed by B.F. Skinner, wherein reinforcement, rather than punishment is the key to behaviour modification (Skinner, 1953).

Positive reinforcement training (PRT) involves rewarding desirable behaviours, such as sitting on command, with treats, praise, or play. Studies reveal that PRT leads to better compliance and emotional well-being in dogs compared to aversive methods. Rooney and Cowan (2011) found that dogs trained using positive reinforcement exhibited lower stress levels and stronger bonds with their guardians.

Evidence-based training prioritises the welfare of the animal. Positive methods minimise stress and fear and create an environment which is conducive to learning. Fear-inducing techniques, often associated with dominance-based training, can result in anxiety, aggression, and other behavioural issues (Herron et al., 2009). Conversely, a science-based framework helps develop trust between dogs and their handlers and paves the way for a cooperative relationship.

Another advantage of evidence-based training lies in its versatility. Techniques rooted in science are adaptable to diverse scenarios, from basic life skills training to specialized tasks such as search-and-rescue operations or assisting individuals with disabilities. For instance, Hobbs et al. (2017) discuss the success of positive reinforcement in training service dogs and show its role in producing reliable and emotionally balanced working animals.

- **The Dominance Theory and Its Origins**

Dominance-based training models stem from the belief that dogs are hierarchically structured animals that require strict control to prevent disobedience. This theory gained prominence in the mid-20th century, heavily influenced by studies of captive wolf packs, which were incorrectly assumed to reflect natural canine social structures (Mech, 1999). These models predominantly rely on aversive methods, which include physical corrections, intimidation, and asserting "alpha" status. Proponents argue that such techniques establish the trainer's authority and prevent behavioural issues. However, subsequent research has debunked many of the foundational assumptions of dominance theory.

One significant flaw is the misinterpretation of social structures in dogs. Modern research reveals that dogs form cooperative, fluid social groups rather than rigid dominance hierarchies. Mech (1999) refuted earlier studies on wolves, noting that familial bonds, rather than dominance, govern pack dynamics. Applying a dominance framework to dog training is scientifically inaccurate and detrimental to canine welfare. Furthermore, dominance-based training often involves punitive measures that can harm dogs both physically and psychologically. Studies have linked such methods to increased stress, fear, and aggression. Herron et al. (2009) reported that dogs subjected to aversive techniques were more likely to exhibit defensive aggression which may pose risks to both the animal and its handler.

From an ethical standpoint, dominance-based training is at odds with contemporary standards for animal welfare. The use of force, intimidation, or pain contradicts the principles of humane treatment and fails to acknowledge dogs' capacity for complex emotions and social learning. Positive, science-based methods offer a more compassionate alternative, emphasising respect for the animal's well-being.

As canine training continues to evolve, ongoing research plays a crucial role in refining methodologies and addressing emerging challenges. Areas such as canine cognition, emotional intelligence, and the impact of training on long-term behaviour warrant further exploration. Integrating advancements in technology, such as wearable devices to monitor stress or reinforcement timing, could enhance the precision and effectiveness of training techniques. Moreover, efforts to educate trainers, veterinarians, and pet guardians about the benefits of science-based approaches are vital. Certification programs and public awareness campaigns can help disseminate accurate information, countering the persistence of dominance-based myths.

Strengthening the Dog-Guardian Bond

The adolescent phase in dogs can test the bond between dogs and their guardians. Building trust and developing effective communication during this stage strengthens the relationship and ensures a harmonious coexistence. Adolescence in dogs parallels that of humans in terms of behavioural challenges. Hormonal changes during puberty influence their mood, energy levels, and responses to stimuli. Many guardians report a decline in life skills during this phase, as previously learned cues are ignored or forgotten. This "teen" phase can also bring about behaviours such as increased reactivity, impulsiveness, and exploration of boundaries (Sommerville et al., 2021). Research highlights that this developmental stage is crucial for social and emotional growth. Guardians who adapt their training and communication strategies to accommodate these changes can reinforce trust and lay a foundation for lifelong companionship (Yin, 2009).

Adolescence may amplify selective hearing or testing of limits but maintaining clear and consistent rules helps the dog handle this confusing stage. For instance, reinforcing basic cues such as "sit" and "stay" and using positive reinforcement techniques ingrain the idea that desired behaviours are rewarding (Ziv, 2017). By avoiding frustration or punitive measures, guardians can help develop an environment where the dog feels secure and supported.

Behavioural regression is common during adolescence. Studies suggest that dogs in this phase may exhibit increased stress or anxiety, leading to temporary setbacks in training (Bray et al., 2021). Guardians should approach these moments with patience, recognizing them as natural developmental hurdles rather than signs of defiance. Gradual, reward-based retraining, paired with ample opportunities for success can rebuild confidence in both the dog and the guardian.

Effective communication during the teenage years often relies on nonverbal cues. Dogs are highly perceptive to human body language, tone, and facial expressions (Kaminski et al., 2017). Guardians can strengthen the bond by adopting open, calm body postures and maintaining soft, encouraging tones. Avoiding confrontational gestures, such as direct staring or aggressive movements helps them develop a sense of safety and trust.

Adolescent dogs may respond differently to cues compared to their puppyhood phase. Short, clear cues paired with immediate rewards, whether treats, play, or affection help develop the desired behaviours. Training sessions should remain brief and engaging to accommodate shorter attention spans (Mills et al., 2005). Interactive play can also enhance communication by creating shared positive experiences. Tug-of-war, fetch, or puzzle toys provide mental stimulation and strengthen the dog-guardian connection. Importantly, play should remain structured to reinforce rules and boundaries.

Adolescence often brings heightened reactivity to new environments, people, or animals. This reactivity is partly a result of fear periods that coincide with puberty. Research suggests that gradual desensitization and counter-conditioning can help manage these reactions (McMillan, 2017). For example, exposing the dog to new stimuli at a comfortable distance, paired with positive reinforcement can reduce fear responses over time.

The teenage phase also marks an increase in exploratory behaviours, which can manifest as ignoring recall cues or escaping boundaries. Consistently practising recall training in low-distraction environments before progressing to busier areas creates the ideal behaviour. Using high-value rewards during these training sessions ensures the dog associates returning to their guardian with a positive outcome (White et al., 2020).

Socialisation during adolescence is as vital as in puppyhood. Positive experiences with other dogs and people help build emotional resilience and prevent fear-based behaviours later in life. Group training classes or controlled playdates offer opportunities for social interaction in a safe, supervised environment (Arhant et al., 2017). Not all dogs experience adolescence in the same way. Factors such as breed, temperament, and past experiences influence their reactions and behaviours. Guardians should adapt their strategies to meet their dog's unique needs, whether by offering more mental stimulation for high-energy breeds or prioritising gentle desensitization for nervous individuals.

Efforts to build trust and communication during adolescence yield long-term benefits. Studies demonstrate that dogs with strong attachments to their guardians are more likely to exhibit secure, well-adjusted behaviours throughout adulthood (Topál et al., 1998). Furthermore, these dogs tend to respond better to training, exhibit lower stress levels, and display fewer behavioural issues.

The teenage years, though challenging, offer an opportunity for guardians to deepen their understanding of their canine companion. By approaching this phase with empathy, consistency, and a commitment to positive reinforcement, the dog-guardian bond can emerge stronger than ever.

CHAPTER 17

THE ADOLESCENT DOG'S DEVELOPMENT

Adolescence is the stage in a dog's life where the dog matures from puppyhood to adulthood and goes through physical and mental maturity. During this time, the male dog experiences a surge in the reproductive hormone known as testosterone, and the female dog experiences an increase in oestrogen, the female reproductive hormone. These hormonal changes induce behavioural changes, such as increased territorial marking, restlessness and mounting. Female dogs enter a cycle, known as the heat cycle which is the start of the reproductive phase.

In addition to hormonal changes, dogs show physical growth which is also a part of adolescence. The skeletal system continues to develop. Some dogs experience growth spurts. While puppies are still growing into adult bodies, the initial signs of adolescent behaviour, such as increased independence and defiance, become evident. For instance, dogs may test boundaries by ignoring cues they previously followed. They mirror the rebellious tendencies observed in human teenagers.

Understanding the Timeline

Understanding the timeline of canine adolescence is essential for managing their development and addressing behavioural challenges effectively. When Does Adolescence Begin? Adolescence in dogs typically begins at approximately 6 months of age, but this starting point can vary significantly based on several factors, including breed, size, and individual temperament. Adolescence is closely tied to puberty when hormonal changes trigger sexual maturity.

The adolescence phase ends when a dog reaches full physical and emotional maturity. This typically happens between 18 and 24 months of age, although the timeline varies widely depending on breed size and other factors. By this stage, dogs achieve their adult size and weight, and their behavioural patterns stabilize. Mature dogs begin to demonstrate improved impulse control and a more consistent temperament. While their behaviour may still require guidance and reinforcement, they generally become more predictable and easier to manage. The exact age at which adolescence ends can vary as small breeds often mature more quickly compared to larger ones.

1. Variations Based on Breed and Size

One of the most critical factors influencing the timeline of canine adolescence is breed size. The differences in growth rates and maturity levels across breeds mean that the duration of adolescence is not uniform for all dogs. Generally, smaller breeds, such as Chihuahuas or Pugs, reach physical and emotional maturity sooner than larger breeds like Great Danes or Saint Bernards.

• Small Breeds

Small breeds typically begin adolescence around 5-6 months and complete it by 12-18 months. These dogs reach their adult size relatively quickly, and their behavioural development often mirrors this accelerated growth. Guardians of small breeds tend to notice that the challenges of adolescence, such as defiant behaviour or heightened energy levels, are shorter-lived compared to larger dogs.

- **Medium Breeds**

Medium-sized breeds, including Cocker Spaniels and Border Collies, usually follow a slightly extended timeline. Adolescence in these breeds generally begins around 6-7 months and ends by 18-20 months. The behavioural changes in medium breeds can be more prolonged and require consistent training and reinforcement throughout this period.

- **Large and Giant Breed**

Large and giant breeds experience the most extended periods of adolescence due to their slower growth rates. For example, Great Danes, Bernese Mountain Dogs, and Mastiffs may begin adolescence around 7-8 months but may not reach full maturity until they are 2-3 years old. It takes them longer to mature because they need more time for their long skeleton and muscular development as well as for them to mature emotionally. Guardians of large breeds need to have the patience to provide their dogs with regular training as well as tackle all the challenges that come with puppies growing into their adolescence.

2. **Variations Based on Individual Temperament**

Beyond breed size, individual temperament also plays a significant role in determining the onset and duration of adolescence. Even within the same breed, some dogs may show early, or late developmental changes based on genetic and environmental factors. Following are some examples.

- **Early Developers**

Certain dogs may start showing signs of adolescence as early as 4-5 months, especially if they are precocious in their physical and hormonal development. Early bloomers may display behaviours such as testing boundaries, increased independence, and heightened curiosity. The well-behaved puppies increasingly start to act stubborn or distracted. To ingrain the desired behaviour in early bloomers, guardians need to reinforce the ideal attitude to prevent undesirable and stubborn behaviour from taking root. Introducing structured activities, regular mental stimulation and gentle guidance help dogs handle this phase. It can also help build a strong foundation for long-term life skills and social behaviour.

- **Late Developers**

Conversely, some dogs may delay the onset of adolescence until they are closer to 8-9 months, particularly in larger breeds or those with slower growth and developmental patterns. These late developers often appear more compliant and easy-going during their early months. The guardians may mistakenly believe they've skipped the challenges of adolescence. However, the behavioural shifts typical of this phase eventually emerge. These dogs may start testing boundaries and become more independent by displaying selective hearing. Guardians should remain prepared and continue to reinforce consistent training and positive behaviours.

- **Temperament Influences**

Individual temperament traits, such as assertiveness, sensitivity, or sociability shape the adolescent experience for each dog. Assertive dogs show heightened stubbornness or a stronger inclination to challenge boundaries and require positive training to maintain control and reinforce good behaviour. On the other hand, sensitive dogs display increased anxiety, stress, or reluctance to engage, and they need a gentler and more reassuring approach to build their confidence. Sociable dogs seek extra interaction and become overly excitable or distracted in social settings.

Physical Growth and Changes

Adolescent dogs experience significant physical transformations as they progress from puppyhood to adulthood. This phase normally begins at around six months and continues until they reach physical maturity. It can vary from breed to breed but generally occurs between 12 to 24 months (Case, 2014). During this period, growth spurts are prominent and are characterised by rapid increases in height and weight, changes in musculature, and the refinement of skeletal structure. These physical developments are influenced by genetics, diet, and overall health.

One of the most noticeable aspects of growth spurts is the rapid elongation of long bones, especially in the legs. This growth contributes to the lanky appearance, which is often seen in adolescent dogs, especially in larger breeds such as Great Danes or German Shepherds (Alexander et al., 2017). The skeletal system undergoes ossification. During this, cartilage transforms into bone and provides the dog with a more robust framework. However, sometimes accelerated growth leads to orthopaedic issues, such as hip dysplasia or growth plate injuries, especially in dogs which are vulnerable to these issues (Bennett & Tennant, 2008).

Muscle development follows skeletal growth, although the two processes are not always synchronised. During this phase, dogs appear awkward and uncoordinated as their muscles adjust to support their rapidly growing bodies (König & Liebich, 2020). Proper nutrition, including adequate protein and calcium levels, is crucial to support both bone and muscle development and to minimise the risk of developmental disorders. Overfeeding or providing excessive nutrients leads to obesity or exacerbates orthopaedic conditions (Laflamme, 2012).

Hormonal changes during adolescence also lead to physical development. The pituitary gland releases growth hormone, which stimulates the growth of tissues and organs. This hormone works in tandem with thyroid hormones and insulin-like growth factor 1 (IGF-1), which are essential for regulating the overall pace of growth (Verstegen et al., 2005).

Imbalances in these hormones can lead to growth abnormalities, such as dwarfism or gigantism.

Sex hormones such as testosterone and oestrogen begin to increase during adolescence. These hormones contribute to the development of secondary sexual characteristics and influence growth plate closure. It leads to the end of longitudinal bone growth (Greer et al., 2007). The timing of growth plate closure varies by breed. The smaller breeds reach this milestone earlier than larger breeds.

The Impact of Sexual Maturity on Behaviour

Sexual maturity typically occurs between six and 12 months of age, depending on the breed and brings about various changes in behaviour. These behavioural shifts are primarily driven by the surge in sex hormones such as testosterone in males and oestrogen in females.

- **Behavioural Changes in Male Dogs**

As testosterone levels rise, male dogs show increased territoriality, mounting behaviours, and roaming tendencies. These behaviours are evolutionary adaptations linked to reproduction, as they enhance the male's ability to locate and compete for mates (Overall, 2013). However, they can also pose challenges for pet guardians, as roaming increases the risk of accidents and exposure to infectious diseases. Training and environmental management, such as secure fencing, are required to mitigate these risks.

Testosterone also influences aggression levels in some male dogs, especially towards other male dogs. This type of aggression is typically associated with competition for mates and is more pronounced in breeds with a history of guarding or fighting roles (Case, 2014). Neutering is often recommended to reduce these behaviours, although its effectiveness varies depending on the dog's age, breed, and individual temperament (McGreevy et al., 2012). Importantly, neutering should be timed carefully, as early neutering has been linked to an increased risk of orthopaedic issues and certain cancers (Hart et al., 2014).

- **Behavioural Changes in Female Dogs**

In females, the onset of oestrus, commonly referred to as "heat," is the start of sexual maturity. Oestrus typically occurs twice a year in most breeds and is accompanied by behavioural changes such as increased vocalization, restlessness, and a heightened interest in male dogs (Reichler, 2009). These behaviours are driven by oestrogen surges and are part of the female's reproductive strategy to attract mates. For guardians who have to manage a female dog in heat can be challenging, as the risk of unintended pregnancies and interactions with male dogs increases significantly during this period. Oestrus also influences social interactions, as females may become more irritable or less tolerant of other dogs during this time. (Serpell, 2017).

Brain Development in Adolescent Dogs

During the adolescent phase, brain development in dogs takes place and significant changes occur in neural structure and function. These changes are largely governed by the maturation of the prefrontal cortex, which is responsible for functions such as focus, impulse control, and decision-making (Dodman & Shuster, 2017). During this stage, the prefrontal cortex is still developing, while other areas of the brain, such as the limbic system, responsible for emotional responses, are more active. This imbalance explains why adolescent dogs often exhibit impulsive behaviours and have difficulty maintaining focus.

Neurotransmitter activity also undergoes significant shifts during adolescence. Dopamine, a neurotransmitter associated with reward and motivation, experiences a surge. This increase in dopamine activity makes adolescent dogs more responsive to novel stimuli and rewards but also increases their susceptibility to distractions (Pereira et al., 2020). The underdeveloped state of the prefrontal cortex means that adolescent dogs often struggle with impulse control. They may act on instinct rather than deliberation which may lead to behaviours such as jumping on guests, chasing moving objects, or stealing food. These behaviours are not indicative of defiance but rather a reflection of the brain's developmental stage. (MacLean et al., 2019).

Additionally, synaptic pruning is a process where unused neural connections are eliminated, and it occurs during adolescence. This process is vital for optimizing brain efficiency but can temporarily disrupt established behaviours and learning patterns. For example, a dog that previously mastered basic cues may suddenly seem less reliable in performing them. This regression is temporary and should be addressed with continued training and reinforcement (Case, 2014).

Understanding the Science of Decision-Making in Teen Dogs

Decision-making in adolescent dogs is influenced by the prefrontal cortex and the limbic system. The limbic system, which includes the amygdala and hippocampus, is fully functional during adolescence and dominates emotional responses and risk assessment. In contrast, the prefrontal cortex, which moderates these responses, is still in the process of maturing. This developmental disparity can result in extreme emotional reactivity and inconsistent decision-making (Overall, 2013).

Adolescent dogs are more likely to engage in risk-taking behaviours, such as exploring unfamiliar areas or interacting with potentially threatening stimuli. It is a tendency which is driven by a combination of increased dopamine activity and an underdeveloped ability to assess consequences. For example, an adolescent dog may dart into a busy street to chase a squirrel and is unable to fully comprehend the danger that is involved in this. (Serpell, 2017).

Research also indicates that adolescent dogs have an increased sensitivity to social cues from both humans and other dogs. Sensitivity is thought to be an adaptive mechanism that facilitates the dog in social learning and integration into social groups. However, it can also lead to increased susceptibility to stress or anxiety in unfamiliar or high-pressure situations. For instance, a teenage dog may misinterpret a benign gesture from another dog as a threat and this can cause reactive behaviours (Reichler, 2009).

Adolescent dogs also show a phenomenon known as "social plasticity," when their brain's neural networks become highly adaptable to social experiences. This type of plasticity makes adolescence an important period for shaping a dog's responses to social and environmental stimuli. Positive experiences during this time lead to well-adjusted adult behaviours, while negative experiences can have lasting adverse effects (Pereira et al., 2020).

Neurochemical changes during adolescence further complicate focus and decision-making. Serotonin, a neurotransmitter associated with mood regulation and impulse control, is in flux during this period. Reduced serotonin activity increases impulsivity and aggression in dogs, which may manifest as sudden outbursts or difficulty adhering to established behavioural norms (Case, 2014). Moreover, oxytocin, often referred to as the "bonding hormone," can enhance bonding with humans and other dogs with increased levels. However, it can also heighten sensitivity to social rejection or conflict. (Dodman & Shuster, 2017).

Emotional and Social Development

Adolescence in dogs is also a time of emotional growth. Emotional regulation is the ability to manage and respond to emotional experiences and tends to be underdeveloped in adolescent dogs. During this phase, they often demonstrate increased sensitivity to stressors and may react unpredictably to new or challenging situations. (Horwitz & Mills, 2009). One of the key strategies for developing emotional regulation in adolescent dogs is gradual exposure to stress-inducing situations. Controlled socialisation experiences, such as meeting unfamiliar dogs or handling noisy environments, help dogs build coping mechanisms. (Case, 2014).

Dogs often struggle with abrupt changes in their environment or schedule, which cause anxiety or behavioural issues. They also struggle with increased fearfulness and anxiety even toward familiar stimuli. The periods of intense anxiety and fearfulness normally resolve after some time, but the guardian must exercise patience and understanding during this time (Overall, 2013). Providing a structured routine with consistent feeding, exercise, and training times creates a sense of security. It also reduces stress and promotes emotional stability (Serpell, 2017). Emotional resilience can also be nurtured through activities that engage the dog's mind and senses. Puzzle toys, scent games, and interactive play challenge the dog cognitively and provide an outlet for excess energy. These activities stimulate the release of endorphins, and promote relaxation and emotional balance (Pereira et al., 2020).

Recognising Your Dog's Social Needs During This Phase

As pack animals, dogs have an inherent need for social interaction, both with humans and other dogs. Adolescence is a critical period for shaping these interactions and ensuring the dog's social needs are met (Horwitz & Mills, 2009).

Puppies typically rely heavily on their primary caregiver for security, but adolescent dogs begin to explore their independence (MacLean et al., 2019). Regular social interactions with other dogs are crucial during adolescence, as they help the dog learn appropriate social behaviours. Supervised play sessions with well-matched canine companions provide opportunities for the dog to practice communication skills such as reading body language, taking turns, and resolving conflicts (Reichler, 2009). Guardians should also be mindful of the quality and frequency of social interactions. Overexposure to poorly managed social situations, such as chaotic dog parks, can overwhelm an adolescent dog and lead to negative associations. Instead, controlled environments where the dog can interact with calm and well-socialised dogs are more beneficial. Gradually increasing the complexity of social scenarios allows the dog to build confidence and adaptability over time (Serpell, 2017).

Consistent, positive engagement with family members reinforces the dog's trust and strengthens the human-animal bond. Activities such as training sessions, grooming, and interactive games help provide valuable opportunities for social bonding while reinforcing the dog's sense of belonging. These interactions should be adjusted to the dog's personality, as some may thrive on active engagement, while others may prefer quieter, one-on-one time with their guardian (Dodman & Shuster, 2017). Adolescent dogs may occasionally need breaks from social interactions, especially if they exhibit behaviours such as avoidance, excessive barking, or snapping. Providing the dog with a safe, quiet space to decompress can help them regain their emotional balance and prepare for future social interactions (Overall, 2013).

Chapter Highlights

- Testosterone and oestrogen surges cause behavioural shifts like marking, restlessness, and mounting.

- Smaller breeds mature faster, while larger breeds take up to 2-3 years to fully develop.

- Dogs experience growth spurts, skeletal development, and muscle coordination challenges.

- Adolescent dogs are sensitive to stress and need structured routines and socialisation.

- Impulse control improves as the prefrontal cortex matures.

CHAPTER 18
CHALLENGES OF CANINE ADOLESCENCE

Dogs undergo various challenges as they grow into puberty. Their behaviour becomes erratic, and often uncontrollable for caregivers. Unable to understand the reasons behind the behavioural quirks of their dog, guardians become frustrated which often convinces them to abandon their dogs to shelters. This is an ad nauseum situation which is a result of ignorance. The behavioural shift that occurs during the adolescent period is due to hormonal and neurological changes taking place in the body.

To create a lasting relationship and bond with the dog, caregivers must be equipped with knowledge about the adolescent phase of dogs, behavioural challenges and quirks that arise during this phase. This is a crucial phase when the dog experiences various stimuli that change his perception of the world and often lead to challenging behaviours like leash-pulling, recall regression, and destructive chewing.

Behavioural Quirks of Teen Dogs

Recent research led by Lucy Asher, a behavioural scientist at Newcastle University's School of Natural and Environmental Sciences, sheds light on the behavioural similarities between adolescent humans and adolescent dogs. The study provides valuable insights into the "teenage" phase of dogs, accompanied by a temporary shift in life skills and attachment behaviours.

The research team focused on guide dog puppies, including breeds like German Shepherds, Labrador Retrievers, Golden Retrievers, and their mixed-breed counterparts. The goal was to explore whether the relationship between dogs and their caregivers mirrors the parent-child dynamic in humans, particularly during adolescence. This period often challenges relationships and behavioural norms. To gather data, the team utilized a combination of behavioural questionnaires and practical tests. Caregivers, acting as parental figures and professional dog trainers completed these questionnaires, which assessed the dogs' life skills and attachment levels. A sample of 285 dogs was included in the survey, while 69 of these dogs underwent additional behavioural testing. Observations were conducted when the dogs were five months old during their preadolescence, eight months old during adolescence, and 12 months old during post-adolescence.

In the questionnaires, obedience was evaluated using statements like "Needs obedience cues repeated to get a response" and "Refuses to obey cues it has previously learned." For the behavioural tests, life skills were measured through the dogs' responses to a familiar command, "Sit!". It is a skill all dogs in the study had mastered in five months. The number of repeated cues needed to elicit the desired response provided a quantitative measure of obedience. The results revealed a noticeable dip in life skills during the adolescent phase at around eight months of age. Compared to their behaviour at five months or 12 months, dogs during this middle stage were more than twice as likely to ignore initial cues, requiring multiple repetitions to comply. Interestingly, this defiance appeared to be selective, directed primarily toward their caregivers. In contrast, trainers or relative strangers faced far less resistance (Coren, 2020).

This selective rebellion aligns with findings from human studies, where adolescent defiance tends to be more pronounced in relationships lacking secure emotional attachment. To explore this connection in dogs, researchers examined the emotional bond between dogs and their caregivers. Indicators of attachment included questions like, "Becomes agitated (whines, jumps up, tries to intervene) when you show affection for another dog or animal." The data confirmed a parallel to human behaviour. Dogs with weaker emotional attachments to their caregivers displayed higher levels of disobedience.

While the adolescent phase brought challenges, it was a temporary period of behavioural turbulence. Lucy Asher emphasised that these changes were short-lived. By the time the dogs reached 12 months, their behaviour generally returned to preadolescent levels or showed improvement. This reassurance is crucial for dog guardians who may feel overwhelmed during this phase. The findings carry significant implications for dog guardians and the broader community. During adolescence, dogs are no longer the endearing, compliant puppies they once were. Instead, their behaviour can become erratic and challenging. It may lead to frustration for guardians. Unfortunately, this is also the phase when many dogs are surrendered to shelters, as guardians struggle to cope with their pet's sudden disobedience.

Moreover, they begin to develop a stronger sense of confidence and curiosity. By this stage, they have become familiar with their routine walks and surroundings, which may lead them to explore further than before. Growing taller allows them to see more of their environment, sparking an increased interest in what lies beyond their usual boundaries. This is often accompanied by behaviours that resemble those of human teenagers, such as ignoring calls from their guardians. These changes are a natural part of development as dogs try to make sense of the world around them and learn through new experiences. For instance, a dog may have discovered the thrill of chasing wildlife in the garden, a habit that could carry over into walks. Similarly, they might realise that running toward another dog can sometimes lead to playful interactions. Studies, including research by Bray et al. (2017), identify this stage as one where life skills tend to decrease while risk-taking behaviours increase.

During adolescence, dogs often experience changes in their social preferences. They may show greater interest in unfamiliar dogs or people, depending on prior experiences, or they might suddenly dislike certain individuals or situations. This phase can also bring about juvenile shyness. As a result, anxiety-related issues might surface, making previously neutral or enjoyable experiences more stressful for the adolescent dog. Unneutered adolescent dogs emit stronger scents due to rising hormone levels, which can attract unwanted attention. These scents might provoke older, nervous, or neutered dogs, resulting in encounters where the adolescent is barked at, snapped at, or lunged at. Such incidents leave a lasting impression and teach young dogs to associate other dogs with fear. This leads to barking or other defensive behaviours when another dog appears.

Adolescent dogs often display erratic energy levels, alternating between bursts of high activity and periods of lethargy. These fluctuations stem from both physical and mental changes occurring during this stage. Around six months of age, many guardians reduce their dog's meals to twice a day and structured activities like puppy training classes often become less frequent. With less one-on-one attention, dogs may feel under-stimulated, which makes them seek out their own entertainment. Unfortunately, this can result in inappropriate behaviours such as digging or destructive chewing. However, the study shows that punishment is not an effective solution. Adolescence in dogs, much like in humans, is a developmental stage that cannot be rushed or disciplined away. Instead, patience and understanding are essential. Recognising this phase as a normal part of growth can help guardians maintain a positive relationship with their dogs and cope with this phase in a better way.

The Hormonal Rollercoaster

Hormonal changes during adolescence in dogs are akin to the emotional and physical challenges faced by human teenagers. As dogs enter puberty, hormonal surges can dramatically influence their behaviour, sometimes in ways that are surprising or even confusing to their guardians. Understanding these changes is crucial for managing this developmental stage effectively.

1. **Hormonal Surges and Their Effects**

For male dogs, puberty brings a significant increase in testosterone levels. This surge often leads to behaviours such as increased marking, where dogs urinate on objects or structures to establish territory or communicate with other dogs. The rise in testosterone may also amplify sniffing and wandering behaviours as males become more attuned to scents in their environment, particularly those of female dogs. This intense sensitivity can result in pulling on the lead and developing a strong desire to explore new areas or even attempts to escape.

For both males and females, the influence of sex hormones often leads to a sense of restlessness. For instance, rising hormone levels can increase body temperatures, causing dogs to experience something similar to human hot flashes. Dogs that were previously content at night might begin vocalising unexpectedly which can disrupt their household. Guardians frequently report dogs whining, barking, or pacing in the middle of the night, despite having been well-adjusted to sleeping alone previously. Upon closer examination, this behaviour is often linked to physical discomfort caused by hormonal fluctuations rather than external factors like noises or disturbances.

2. Female Dogs and the First Oestrous Cycle

Female dogs typically experience their first oestrous cycle, or heat, around seven months of age, although this timing can vary depending on the breed and individual factors. This period marks the onset of significant hormonal and behavioural changes. Some female dogs may become more lethargic and display a strong need for closeness with their guardian to seek reassurance and security during this unfamiliar phase. Conversely, others may exhibit bolder or more defensive behaviours. Increased vocalisations are common, and some females may collect and guard objects by displaying a possessive streak that was not previously evident. Sensitivity to touch can also increase, and some dogs may react defensively when other dogs approach them. On the other hand, some females become unusually sociable and require interaction with other dogs more frequently than before. Guardians often observe mood swings or sudden shifts in temperament. For instance, a normally relaxed dog may become irritable or overly excitable. These changes are typically temporary and closely tied to the hormonal ebbs and flows of the oestrous cycle (Maclean, et al. 2019).

3. The Effects of Spaying and Neutering During Adolescence

Spaying and neutering dogs have long been associated with reducing unwanted behaviours, controlling pet populations, and mitigating aggression. However, extensive research reveals a more complex picture, particularly regarding behavioural outcomes following these procedures during adolescence. Studies by Deborah L. Duffy and James A. Serpell, as well as Parvene Farhoody, challenge traditional beliefs about the behavioural benefits of spaying and neutering.

Both the Duffy and Serpell study and Farhoody's research utilised the Canine Behavioural Assessment and Research Questionnaire (C-BARQ). This tool, developed by Serpell and colleagues, provides a comprehensive assessment of canine behaviour across 101 metrics, including aggression, fear, anxiety, attachment, excitability, and energy levels. The reliability of this method stems from structured input provided directly by dog guardians, capturing real-world behaviour in various settings. The datasets analysed in these studies are extensive. Duffy and Serpell evaluated a combined total of 5,145 dogs, while Farhoody's research included 10,839 dogs. With 15,984 dogs assessed overall, these studies represent one of the largest and most robust examinations of the behavioural impacts of spaying and neutering to date.

One of the most startling findings from these studies is that spayed and neutered dogs exhibit significantly higher levels of aggression than their intact counterparts. This result is counterintuitive, given that aggression reduction is often cited as a reason for performing these procedures. Across the studies, aggression increased by 20% to more than double, depending on the specific type e.g., guardian-directed or stranger-directed aggression. Interestingly, an increase in aggression was observed in both males and females. However, for females, the timing of the procedure appeared to play a crucial role. Early spaying, defined as occurring before the dog reached one year of age, was associated with a significantly higher increase in aggression compared to later spaying. Male dogs, in contrast, exhibited increased aggression regardless of the age at which they were neutered.

The studies also revealed an approximately 31% increase in fearfulness among spayed and neutered dogs. This increased fear response extended across various stimuli and made the dogs more reactive to their environment. Additionally, touch sensitivity which is a measure of discomfort or aversion to being handled increased by 33% in both sexes. These changes suggest that hormonal alterations following spaying or neutering may play a role in amplifying a dog's anxiety and defensive behaviours.

Another noteworthy finding was an 8% rise in excitability among spayed and neutered dogs. This increase reflects a tendency for these dogs to react more intensely to stimuli, making them less predictable and potentially more difficult to manage in everyday situations. Farhoody's findings also indicated that neutered dogs were generally less trainable than intact dogs, further complicating their behaviour. This contradicts the commonly held belief that spaying and neutering enhance a dog's temperament and trainability. One of the few positive behavioural changes associated with spaying and neutering was a substantial decrease in urine marking. The studies found a 68% reduction in this behaviour, which can be a significant benefit for guardians managing dogs prone to territorial marking. However, this benefit must be weighed against the broader behavioural changes observed.

The idea that spaying and neutering solve behavioural problems has been ingrained in dog training and veterinary advice for decades. However, these studies reveal that for most behavioural issues, the procedures may worsen outcomes. Duffy and Serpell's conclusion, "For most behaviours, spaying/neutering was associated with worse behaviour, contrary to conventional wisdom," demonstrates the need for a more nuanced understanding of these interventions. While the data from these studies is robust, additional research is necessary to fully under-stand the mechanisms driving these behavioural changes. Hormonal shifts, environmental factors, and genetic predispositions likely interact in complex ways, contributing to the observed outcomes. Future studies could explore strategies to mitigate the negative behavioural effects of spaying and neutering or investigate alternative approaches to managing reproduction and behaviour in dogs.

Common Challenges and How to Address Them

Destructive behaviour in dogs can arise from several underlying causes. While some instances are related to natural and developmental processes, others are linked to environmental or emotional factors that require attention.

- **Recall Regression**

Adolescent dogs often exhibit a decline in their previously reliable ability to respond to recall cues, a phenomenon commonly referred to as recall regression. This behavioural challenge is attributed to a combination of developmental, hormonal, and environmental factors (Hoffman et al., 2014). During adolescence, dogs undergo significant neurological and hormonal changes that impact their behaviour and learning. Increased independence and curiosity are hallmarks of this stage, often leading to a reduction in responsiveness to training cues.

Research highlights the role of hormonal fluctuations in recall regression. For instance, unneutered adolescent dogs may exhibit heightened interest in exploring their environment, driven by the surge of gonadal hormones (Landsberg et al., 2013). These hormones can amplify exploratory behaviours, making external stimuli such as scents or other animals more compelling than the guardian's recall command. Environmental distractions further compound the issue. Adolescent dogs are particularly sensitive to novel stimuli during this stage, as their sensory processing and cognitive development are still maturing (Horowitz et al., 2020). The novelty of stimuli like unfamiliar scents or moving objects can override previously learned cues, reflecting the competition between internal motivation and external distractions. Another factor influencing recall regression is the association of recall cues with undesirable outcomes, such as the end of playtime. Dogs are capable of associating recall with the cessation of enjoyable activities, which can decrease their motivation to respond (Range et al., 2008). Additionally, changes in the brain's prefrontal cortex during adolescence may reduce impulse control, further contributing to behavioural inconsistency (Sánchez et al., 2017).

- **Leash-Pulling**

Leash-pulling is another common behavioural issue seen in adolescent dogs. This behaviour occurs when a dog pulls on the leash during walks, often causing frustration and physical strain for the handler. Research has identified several underlying factors for this behaviour, including the dog's developmental stage, energy levels, and environmental triggers (Overall, 2013). Adolescent dogs often experience a surge in energy and enthusiasm, which can lead to impulsive behaviours such as pulling on the leash. According to Landsberg et al. (2013), this stage of development is marked by an increase in exploratory behaviour, which is influenced by both hormonal and environmental factors. Dogs at this age are driven to investigate their surroundings, making them more likely to pull toward stimuli such as other animals, people, or novel objects.

Inconsistencies in leash training also contribute to the persistence of leash-pulling. When dogs occasionally succeed in reaching their goal by pulling, this behaviour is positively reinforced, making it more likely to recur (Overall, 2013). Furthermore, the physical strength of adolescent dogs increases significantly during this stage, making their pulling more forceful and harder to control for handlers (Sánchez et al., 2017). External stimuli, such as the sight of a squirrel or another dog, act as powerful motivators for leash-pulling. Dogs in adolescence are particularly attuned to their environment, often becoming fixated on stimuli that elicit instinctual responses (Landsberg et al., 2013). This fixation can lead to intense pulling episodes as the dog attempts to reach the source of their interest.

- **Chewing:**

Often, puppies engage in chewing as part of their natural development, alleviating the discomfort of teething. Adult dogs, on the other hand, may chew out of boredom, stress, or anxiety, particularly if left alone without adequate stimulation. Chewing is an instinctive behaviour for dogs. Many enjoy gnawing on bones or toys like a Kong stuffed with their favourite treat. This activity satisfies their innate need to chew and provides mental and physical stimulation. Offering dogs appropriate items to chew on can significantly reduce the likelihood of them damaging household items. Providing healthy and safe chew toys helps channel their natural tendencies constructively and makes it easier for guardians to manage any unwanted behaviour.

Dogs left alone for extended periods without stimulation often resort to chewing as a way to alleviate boredom or stress. Addressing this behaviour requires understanding the circumstances in which it occurs. As many dog behaviourists explain, managing destructive chewing requires both prevention strategies and direct intervention. For those unable to supervise their dogs consistently, it is important to create an environment where the dog feels secure and engaged is essential.

Understanding why adult dogs chew requires a bit more investigation. Unlike puppies, whose chewing is primarily driven by teething, adult dogs may chew for a variety of reasons. Stress, boredom, and anxiety are common triggers. For some dogs, changes in their environment or routine, such as a new baby, changes in work schedules, or the loss of a companion lead to destructive behaviours.

Separation anxiety is one of the leading causes of excessive chewing and destructive behaviour in adult dogs. Dogs suffering from this condition often struggle with being left alone, displaying behaviours such as chewing, digging, or excessive barking. Changes in the household, such as the addition or loss of a family member or pet, can exacerbate this anxiety. Although separation anxiety can affect puppies, it tends to become more apparent as dogs mature and settle into adult routines. Dogs with a predisposition to anxiety may require more tailored approaches to feel secure when left alone.

Strategies to Address Destructive Behaviours

Separation anxiety and destructive behaviour in dogs can be challenging for pet guardians, but with consistent strategies and a focus on understanding your dog's needs, these behaviours can be managed effectively. By creating calm, structured routines and providing mental and physical stimulation, guardians can help their dogs feel more secure and reduce unwanted behaviours.

- **Calmn Departures and Homecomings:**

One of the most effective strategies for managing separation anxiety in dogs is to ensure that departures and homecomings remain calm and low-key. Overly enthusiastic greetings or emotional goodbyes can inadvertently heighten a dog's stress and make separations more challenging. Instead, when returning home, guardians should avoid acknowledging their dog immediately, giving the pet time to settle and display calm behaviour, such as sitting quietly. Once the dog is relaxed, offering a gentle stroke and using soothing words reinforces the desired calm demeanour. This approach helps the dog associate homecoming with stability and reduces the anxiety linked to separations over time.

- **Creating Emotional and Physical Space:**

For dogs that struggle with anxiety or over-attachment, establishing some emotional and physical distance is a crucial step in promoting independence. One practical measure is to prevent the dog from accessing the sofa or bed at night. This simple adjustment helps set clear boundaries and develops a healthier dynamic between the dog and the guardian. Providing the dog with a comfortable alternative, such as a designated bed in a safe space, reinforces this sense of independence. After approximately three months, depending on the dog's progress in managing anxiety and adjusting to these changes, the restrictions can be reassessed and gradually relaxed if appropriate.

- **Reducing Shadowing Behaviour:**

Dogs that constantly follow their guardians around the house, even to the bathroom, display excessive attachment or anxiety. To address this, guardians can practice simple cues like "Sit" and "Stay," gradually increasing the distance and time the dog is left in another room. Closing doors behind them when leaving a room further reinforces this independence. Over time, the dog will learn that it is okay to be alone, even briefly, without constant access to the guardian.

- **Introducing Short Alone Periods:**

Helping a dog become comfortable being alone starts with short, positive experiences. Providing a stuffed Kong filled with healthy, moist food can be an excellent distraction. Guardians can experiment with nutritious brands like Forthglade, which many dogs enjoy. Breaking this into three to six short sessions per day allows the dog to associate being left alone with a rewarding experience. For additional plans, working with a behaviour specialist can provide additional support.

- **The Rapid Returns Technique:**

An effective technique for managing separation anxiety in dogs is the "Rapid Returns" method. This approach involves the guardian leaving the dog in a room for a brief period, such as one to two minutes, and then returning without engaging or acknowledging the dog. This lack of attention upon return reinforces the idea that departures and arrivals are neutral events, reducing the emotional intensity surrounding them. Gradually increasing the duration of these absences helps the dog acclimate to being alone, building their confidence and reducing stress. Consistent repetition allows the dog to associate being left alone with safety and security. Over time, this method fosters a calmer response to separations, helping the dog become more independent and self-assured.

- **Managing the Dog's Environment:**

Limiting a dog's access to specific areas of the home when unsupervised is an effective way to prevent damage and promote calm behaviour. Creating a safe zone, a warm, dry, well-lit area such as a kitchen or hallway equipped with a comfortable bed, can provide security and encourage the dog to settle. While well-trained dogs may have earned the freedom to roam, those exhibiting destructive tendencies benefit from restricted access to reduce the risk of accidents or mischief. Dogs should not be left alone for more than four hours without a break, as extended isolation can lead to anxiety and behavioural issues. For longer absences, guardians should consider hiring a professional dog walker, enlisting a neighbour, or arranging for someone to check on the dog, providing companionship and a necessary toilet break.

- **Using Food for Enrichment:**

Food-based enrichment is an effective way to keep dogs mentally and physically occupied. Items like stuffed Kongs or interactive toys such as the Kong Wobbler can engage a dog for extended periods. Frozen treats or raw bones can provide additional stimulation, but guardians must supervise to ensure safety. Choosing high-quality, traceable food or bones, ideally from organic or pasture-raised sources, ensures the dog receives proper nutrition. For households with multiple dogs, feeding bones separately can prevent competition and potential aggression.

- **Mental Stimulation and Activities:**

Beyond food-based distractions, providing mental stimulation through training and interactive play is essential for a dog's overall well-being. Engaging a dog's mind can reduce boredom, alleviate stress, and foster better behaviour. Resources such as *Brain Games for Dogs* offer numerous creative ideas to keep dogs occupied and mentally challenged, ranging from puzzle toys to hide-and-seek games. Structured activities like agility, flyball, tracking, or herding cater to a dog's natural instincts and help burn off excess energy. These activities are especially beneficial for high-energy breeds or those bred for specific tasks, such as herding or retrieving. By incorporating regular mental and physical challenges, guardians can enrich their dog's daily life and strengthen the bond they share with their pets.

- **Preparing the Home Before Leaving:**

Before leaving, guardians should thoroughly dog-proof their homes to minimise risks and prevent destructive behaviour. Items like shoes, remote controls, laundry, and children's toys should be removed from areas the dog can access, as these can easily tempt a bored pet. Waste bins should also be kept out of reach or secured with pet-proof lids, as they can become a source of fascination and lead to messes or ingestion of harmful items. Additionally, any fragile or valuable items should be placed out of reach. By ensuring the home is free from hazards and temptations, guardians can prevent expensive accidents, injuries, or damage.

- **Responding to Damage or Messes:**

If a dog causes damage or creates a mess while alone, it is important for guardians to remain calm and avoid reprimanding the dog. Dogs do not act out of malice or spite; their behaviour is often a response to stress, boredom, or unmet needs. Punishing a dog after the fact is ineffective because they cannot associate the punishment with their earlier actions. Instead, guardians should focus on calmly cleaning up the mess and reevaluating the dog's environment, routine, or management strategies. Identifying triggers such as insufficient exercise, lack of mental stimulation, or too much-unsupervised freedom can guide necessary adjustments. By addressing these gaps proactively, guardians can prevent future incidents and develop healthier, happier relationships with their pets.

- **Seeking Professional Support:**

For persistent behavioural challenges, consulting a dog behaviour specialist is highly recommended. Specialists can provide tailored advice and strategies designed to address the root causes of destructive behaviour and separation anxiety. These professionals evaluate the dog's environment, routine, and specific triggers to create a customized plan that works for both the pet and the guardian. By employing patience, consistency, and appropriate tools, most cases of unwanted behaviours can be successfully resolved. Dogs thrive in structured, supportive environments where their physical and emotional needs are met.

Chapter Highlights

- Adolescent dogs often display erratic energy levels, alternating between bursts of high activity and periods of lethargy.

- Guardians frequently report dogs whining, barking, or pacing in the middle of the night, despite having been well-adjusted to sleeping alone previously.

- Hormonal surges, particularly in male and female dogs, significantly influence behaviours like marking, leash-pulling, and mood swings.

- Structured routines, positive reinforcement, and mental stimulation are essential strategies for managing adolescent behaviours effectively.

- Spaying and neutering during adolescence can have unexpected behavioural consequences, such as increased aggression and anxiety, requiring careful consideration.

CHAPTER 19

POSITIVE GUIDANCE FOR GUARDIANS

For centuries, dogs' trainings were dominance and obedience based which negatively impacted dog's health and emotional well-being. Science has revealed the benefits of positive training methods and the complexity of canine emotions and cognition. Starting your life by adopting a dog requires patience as the dog continues to grow. The ideal relationship between the guardian and the dog is built on trust. No matter how many bumps come along the way, if the pet parents exercise patience, they will inevitably develop a rewarding relationship.

Beyond cues and tricks, training becomes an opportunity to celebrate the unique spirit of each dog. It's about embracing their quirks, developing their confidence, and cultivating a relationship built on understanding rather than fear. This isn't just an evolution in training, it's a revolution in how we view our four-legged companions and the depth of their roles in our lives.

Training with Kindness and Science

The debate on dog training methods has transcended philosophical discussions to become a deeply evidence-based conversation rooted in canine science. Research has unveiled the risks associated with aversive training methods, such as shock collars, prong collars, hitting, and leash corrections, including intense fear, anxiety, stress, aggression, and even damaged relationships between dogs and their guardians (Herron et al., 2009; Rooney & Cowan, 2011; Ziv, 2017; Vieira de Castro et al., 2019). On the other hand, studies show the greater efficacy of positive reinforcement methods. For instance, research indicates that positive reinforcement is more effective than shock collars in teaching dogs to respond to cues such as coming when called (China et al., 2020).

The modern lens through which dog training is viewed prioritises the absence of cruelty and the presence of positive emotional experiences. As Mellor (2016) and Mellor et al. (2020) have emphasised, good animal welfare extends beyond basic needs to include opportunities for positive emotions and experiences. Reward-based training exemplifies this principle by being an enjoyable and enriching activity for dogs. Training sessions using positive reinforcement often incorporate delicious treats or engaging play sessions, making the experience inherently rewarding for the animal. These methods provide cognitive enrichment and strengthen the bond between the dog and its guardian and create a training environment that encourages trust and mutual respect.

A significant societal shift in how dogs are perceived has further influenced training preferences. In contemporary households, dogs are often regarded as family members. They share intimate spaces with their guardians, from lounging on couches to sleeping on beds. These are practices which were once considered taboo by traditional dog trainers. This evolving dynamic reflects the emotional significance of pets in human lives and the recognition of their integral role within the family unit. Inflicting pain or fear on a family member in the name of training feels fundamentally wrong to many people. This sentiment aligns with a growing aversion to aversive training methods, driven by an empathetic understanding of dogs as sentient beings deserving of compassion and care. The shift from viewing dogs as mere subordinates to valuing them as cherished companions reinforces the preference for humane, reward-based training approaches.

The proliferation of canine science has advanced academic understanding and informed the general public. Studies on dog training methods and the remarkable capabilities of dogs, such as detecting diseases like COVID-19—frequently garner widespread media attention. Publications in reputable outlets, such as *Science*, and coverage of topics like pet welfare during the pandemic have made scientific insights more accessible to dog enthusiasts. These articles, often shared widely on social media, contribute to an informed community of dog guardians who are increasingly aware of their pets' needs.

While the internet and popular media still host misinformation, the quality of available resources about dog behaviour and training has improved. Dog lovers are now more equipped to discern evidence-based practices, making them proactive advocates for their pets' well-being. This enhanced awareness, coupled with the societal shift toward treating dogs as family, drives demand for training methods that prioritise the welfare and happiness of dogs.

Dog training has historically been an unregulated profession, allowing anyone to self-identify as a dog trainer without formal qualifications. However, in recent years, there has been a significant shift in the field, with more dog trainers acquiring education that emphasises the use of reward-based methods. These professionals stay current with advancements in canine science, frequently attending conferences, workshops, and training programs led by experts in animal behaviour, veterinary behaviourists, and scientists. Some even pursue academic research and contribute directly to the growing body of knowledge on humane and effective training methods. As a result, there is a growing pool of dog trainers who are both skilled and competent in using reward-based approaches, benefiting dogs and their guardians alike. The increasing professionalism among dog trainers is fuelled by a broader awareness of the importance of evidence-based practices. Many trainers now seek certifications from reputable organizations that emphasise humane training techniques, such as the Karen Pryor Academy, the Certification Council for Professional Dog Trainers (CCPDT), or the International Association of Animal Behaviour Consultants (IAABC).

Attending workshops and conferences has also become a standard practice among dedicated trainers. These events provide opportunities for trainers to learn from experts and stay informed about the latest research in animal behaviour and training methods. For example, studies show that reward-based training methods are not only more effective than aversive techniques but also lead to better welfare outcomes for dogs (Ziv, 2017; Vieira de Castro et al., 2019). Moreover, one of the most promising developments in dog training is the increased accessibility of reward-based trainers. In the past, finding a competent dog trainer often depended on geographic location. Those living in areas without reputable trainers had limited options, often resorting to ineffective or harmful training methods. However, the rise of virtual consultations accelerated by the COVID-19 pandemic has revolutionised the field, offering pet guardians access to qualified trainers regardless of their location. It has provided that virtual consultations can be just as effective as in-person sessions. Research supports the efficacy of remote training programs, which allow trainers to guide dog guardians through reward-based techniques while observing the dog's behaviour in its natural environment (China et al., 2020).

Despite these advancements, challenges remain. Instances of aversive training methods, which rely on fear and pain, persist in some areas.

However, there is growing public awareness about the detrimental effects of such techniques, including increased aggression, anxiety, and stress in dogs (Herron et al., 2009; Rooney & Cowan, 2011). Advocates for humane training are increasingly vocal, using platforms like social media and publications to educate others about the benefits of positive reinforcement. The cultural shift toward humane training methods reflects a broader change in how society views dogs. Pet guardians are increasingly prioritising their dogs' happiness and well-being, often viewing them as integral members of the family. Books like 'Wag: The Science of Making Your Dog Happy' have played a role in spreading this message, emphasising that a dog's happiness, not just life skills should be the ultimate goal of training.

Adolescence in dogs is characterised by a strong desire for independence and exploration. Teenage dogs find the world around them incredibly exciting, which often results in problematic behaviours such as running up to other dogs, jumping on people, or stealing food from kitchen counters. These behaviours, if left unchecked, can persist into adulthood. Preventing undesirable behaviours through effective management is essential to setting teenage dogs up for long-term success.

Management strategies are not a sign of failure but a practical tool for ensuring that dogs do not practice or reinforce unwanted behaviours. For example, using a lead or long-line can prevent dogs with poor recall from running off and disturbing others. Similarly, a baby gate can restrict access to certain areas, like the kitchen, where food theft might occur. Such preventative measures reduce stress for dog guardians and create an environment conducive to successful training. Studies have shown that dogs learn more effectively in structured environments where undesirable behaviours are less likely to be rewarded accidentally (Ziv, 2017; Vieira de Castro et al., 2019). By removing opportunities for reinforcement of unwanted actions, management allows training efforts to focus on teaching and reinforcing desirable behaviours instead. For instance, when a dog cannot steal food or jump on visitors, guardians can concentrate on rewarding polite behaviour and encouraging positive associations and habits.

Adolescent dogs thrive on fun and play, making it essential to incorporate enjoyment into training sessions. Training is not just about achieving specific goals; it is an opportunity to bond with your dog, build trust, and establish a positive relationship. When training is treated as a game, dogs are naturally more engaged and willing to participate. Pressuring dogs to meet training goals can backfire, particularly during adolescence, when attention spans are shorter, and frustration thresholds are lower. If training feels like a chore to either the guardian or the dog, progress will stall, and both parties may lose motivation. Conversely, viewing training as an enjoyable activity can transform it into a shared experience that both the dog and the guardian look forward to.

Play-based training methods, such as using toys or throwing treats for the dog to chase, are particularly effective in maintaining a dog's focus and enthusiasm. Research supports the use of play as a motivator, showing that it strengthens the bond between dogs and their guardians while promoting better learning outcomes (Rooney & Cowan, 2011; Hiby et al., 2004). Tricks like "paw" or "spin" can be great alternatives to more rigorous life skills tasks when training starts to feel monotonous. These tricks are not only fun but also reinforce the idea that training with the guardian is a positive experience.

Socialisation Done Right

Socialisation is one of the most critical aspects of raising a well-adjusted and confident dog, particularly during adolescence. This period, often characterised by increased curiosity and energy, is also when dogs begin refining their social skills. Teenage dogs are often social butterflies, eager to explore their environment and interact with others. However, they are still learning how to behave appropriately in various social situations, whether with other dogs or with people. Thoughtful socialisation during this phase can shape their behaviour and confidence for a lifetime.

Adolescence is a developmental stage where dogs experience physical and hormonal changes, often resulting in fluctuating behaviour. It is also a sensitive period for learning, where positive social experiences can reinforce desirable behaviours, while negative ones may contribute to fear or aggression later in life (Arhant et al., 2010). Without proper socialisation, adolescent dogs may develop behavioural issues such as fearfulness, reactivity, or excessive excitability. By exposing them to a variety of people, animals, environments, and experiences, guardians can help their dogs build resilience and adaptability, essential traits for a well-rounded adult dog.

Effective Ways to Socialise Your Adolescent Dog

Following are some structured and enjoyable methods to provide positive social experiences for teenage dogs:

- **Group or Solo Hikes:** Exploring new trails introduces dogs to diverse sights, sounds, and smells while building their confidence in unfamiliar settings. Group hikes offer opportunities for social interactions with both humans and dogs.

- **Group Dog Life skills or Agility Classes:** Structured classes provide a controlled environment where dogs can practice social skills and life skills while interacting with others. Research shows that reward-based group training improves both socialisation and the bond between dogs and their guardians (Hiby et al., 2004).

- **Playdates with Dogs and People:** Organising supervised play sessions with friendly dogs of different breeds, ages, and sizes allows your dog to learn appropriate play behaviours and communication skills.

- **Exposure to New Environments:** Taking your dog to places like home improvement stores, dog-friendly parties, parks, or pet supply stores helps them adapt to novel environments. Praise and reward your dog for calm behaviour to reinforce positive associations.

- **Visits to Dog Parks:** Dog parks can be excellent for socialisation but require careful monitoring. Look for well-maintained parks with a mix of well-socialised dogs and avoid overcrowded or chaotic environments.

During adolescence, it is not uncommon for dogs to get into minor scuffles during play sessions, at daycare, or at dog parks. While these incidents may alarm guardians, they are often a normal part of a dog's social learning. Minor disagreements help dogs establish boundaries and understand social cues. If the interaction resolves naturally without significant human intervention, there is no need for concern. However, if scuffles escalate into fights or cause anxiety for the guardian, it is important not to isolate the dog from social interactions altogether. Total isolation can hinder the dog's social development and may lead to increased reactivity or fearfulness. Instead, guardians can opt for more structured socialisation opportunities, such as walking in a group with other dogs and their guardians. They can allow dogs to socialise calmly without the intensity of direct play and closely monitored play sessions with a compatible dog. Moreover, they can provide a safe space for social interaction and learning. Adolescence is also an ideal time to enrol your dog in a training course. Structured training classes reinforce life skills and provide a platform for supervised socialisation. Participating in group classes can reduce stress for guardians while equipping their dogs with the skills to deal with social situations confidently. Making training sessions fun and interactive helps maintain the dog's engagement and motivation. Reward-based training techniques are particularly effective during adolescence, as they encourage positive associations and strengthen the bond between the dog and the guardian (Ziv, 2017). By combining training with socialisation, guardians can set their adolescent dogs up for long-term success.

Setting Boundaries with Kindness

The concept of kindness as a transformative force in shaping behaviour finds its roots in behaviourism, a psychological framework championed by B.F. Skinner. Behaviourism emphasises observable behaviours and their modification through reinforcement, with a focus on positive reinforcement to influence actions and develop trust-based relationships. Though sometimes misunderstood, this approach holds implications for animal training, human interactions, and broader ethical considerations.

Kindness, demonstrated through positive reinforcement, has emerged as a scientifically validated and humane method for influencing behaviour. Positive reinforcement rewards desirable actions, encouraging their repetition while avoiding the negative consequences often associated with punishment. This approach develops cooperation and respect, creating relationships rooted in mutual trust. Skinner's experiments with operant conditioning demonstrated that animals, like humans, are more likely to repeat behaviours that lead to positive outcomes (Skinner, 1938).

The efficacy of positive reinforcement lies in its alignment with the natural tendencies of sentient beings to seek rewards and avoid harm. Unlike coercive methods, positive reinforcement motivates learning and engagement without inducing stress or fear. This method is widely used in animal training, including complex cases such as teaching dolphins complex behaviours in aquatic shows or rehabilitating animals with behavioural issues. Studies support the idea that animals trained with positive reinforcement display a greater willingness to learn, improved problem-solving skills, and stronger bonds with their trainers (Ziv, 2017; Vieira de Castro et al., 2019). Central to this kindness-centred approach is the recognition of animals as sentient beings with unique needs, emotions, and motivations. When humans view animals as partners in a shared journey rather than subordinates to control, a deeper understanding of their behaviour emerges (Hiby et al., 2004).

One of the most compelling arguments for positive reinforcement is its effectiveness in achieving long-term behavioural changes. Unlike punishment, which may suppress unwanted behaviours temporarily but often lead to fear or mistrust, positive reinforcement promotes lasting learning and engagement. Animals trained through kindness are more confident and better equipped to adapt to new situations. This principle has been successfully applied across various contexts. For instance, service animals trained using positive reinforcement techniques exhibit reliability in their tasks and a strong bond with their handlers. Similarly, zoo animals trained for medical procedures using positive reinforcement display reduced stress, allowing for safer and more efficient care (Foster & Smith, 2009). Such applications demonstrate the versatility and effectiveness of kindness-centred behaviour modification.

Exercise and Enrichment for Teen Dogs

Understanding and fulfilling a dog's exercise and enrichment needs is a cornerstone of responsible pet guardianship, particularly during adolescence. This phase often marks the peak of a dog's physical and mental energy levels, making it essential for guardians to provide appropriate outlets to prevent frustration and undesirable behaviours. Both physical exercise and mental stimulation play critical roles in a dog's overall well-being and incorporating them into daily routines ensures a balanced and happy life for canine companions.

The amount and type of physical exercise a dog requires depend significantly on factors such as breed, age, and health. Adolescent dogs, in particular, often exhibit high energy levels and require consistent physical activity to burn off excess energy. For example, high-energy breeds like Labrador Retrievers often need 60–90 minutes of vigorous exercise daily to maintain physical health and mental stability. Activities such as running, fetch, swimming, or hiking can help meet these demands, ensuring the dog remains physically fit and mentally engaged.

In contrast, brachycephalic breeds such as French Bulldogs require a more cautious approach. These breeds are prone to respiratory issues and heat sensitivity which limit their capacity for intense exercise (Packer et al., 2015). Guardians of such breeds should prioritise shorter, low-intensity activities to ensure that their dogs remain active without risking their health. Monitoring individual tolerance levels and adapting exercise routines accordingly is necessary for preventing exhaustion or injury.

The benefits of adequate physical exercise extend beyond physical health. Regular activity has been shown to reduce stress, improve sleep quality, and minimise behavioural issues such as hyperactivity or destructive chewing (O'Haire, 2013). For adolescent dogs, structured exercise provides a constructive outlet for their energy, reducing the likelihood of frustration-driven behaviours. Equally important as physical exercise is mental enrichment, which taps into a dog's natural instincts and cognitive abilities. Dogs are highly intelligent animals and are capable of solving complex problems and learning advanced skills. Providing opportunities for mental stimulation prevents boredom and strengthens the bond between dogs and their guardians.

Puzzle toys are a simple and effective way to incorporate mental stimulation into a dog's routine. These toys challenge dogs to work for their food or treats and help them engage their problem-solving skills. Another approach is incorporating scent work, agility, or herding activities, which align with the natural instincts of many breeds. Research has demonstrated that enrichment activities enhance a dog's mental well-being and can significantly reduce stress-related behaviours (Clark et al., 2018).

A practical way to enrich a dog's daily life is to replace traditional bowl feeding with mealtime games. For example, placing meals in a puzzle toy or scattering kibble in the yard encourages dogs to use their noses and brains to "hunt" for food. Training sessions that reinforce basic cues like "sit," "stay," or "come" also double as mental stimulation and promote life skills while keeping dogs mentally engaged. One of the most important skills to teach any dog is reliable recall. This behaviour ensures a dog's safety and provides the freedom to explore off-leash environments under controlled conditions. Training recall requires patience, consistency, and positive reinforcement.

To begin, the recall cue, typically "Come!", should be associated with a positive outcome. In a quiet, distraction-free environment, the cue word is said cheerfully, followed by an immediate reward with a high-value treat, such as cheese, chicken, or beef liver. This exercise is repeated multiple times until the dog shows excitement upon hearing the cue. Once the dog recognises the cue, recall can be practised indoors by adding movement. The dog is called while the handler runs away in an enthusiastic manner. When the dog reaches the handler, they are rewarded with a treat or a fun game like tug or fetch. For shy or nervous dogs, movements can be adjusted to avoid overwhelming them, opting for slower, more inviting gestures. Repetition and variation in rewards are key to maintaining enthusiasm during training.

After mastering recall indoors, the next step is transitioning to a low-distraction outdoor setting, such as a backyard. A 4–6-foot leash ensures control, while the cue continues to be reinforced with high-value rewards. Calling the dog from short distances and gradually increasing the challenge as their confidence and focus improve are essential during this stage. The final stage involves practising recall in high-distraction areas like parks. A long training line (15–30 feet) provides the dog more freedom while maintaining safety. It is crucial to have a treat pouch stocked with the dog's favourite rewards and to be patient as they handle new distractions. Gradually increasing the complexity of the environment and reinforcing successes with consistent rewards ensures progress.

Greeting people is an exciting event for dogs, often leading to behaviours like jumping, pulling, or mouthing. Teaching appropriate greeting behaviour ensures that dogs remain polite and manageable during interactions. To achieve this, preparation is key. Equip yourself with a leash, treats, and, optionally, a mat or rug. Keeping the dog on a leash helps maintain control during training. Start by asking the dog to "sit" and focus on you, praising and rewarding them for their calm behaviour. As you approach a person or allow them to approach slowly, maintain a loose leash and use positive verbal reinforcement, such as "Good!" to encourage calmness. If the dog pulls on the leash or jumps, immediately take two steps back and create distance from the person. This teaches that undesirable behaviour delays the reward of greeting. When the leash is loose and the dog's attention is back on you, resume the approach, maintaining focus with verbal cues and name recognition. Upon reaching the person, ask the dog to "sit" or "sit and stay," rewarding this calm behaviour by allowing a brief greeting. Keep these interactions short, as prolonged greetings may overexcite the dog. If the dog jumps or mouths the person, calmly back them away or have the person step back. Reset the exercise and try again.

An alternative approach is place training, where the dog learns to go to a designated spot, such as a mat or bed when guests arrive. This can begin by meeting guests outside with the dog on a leash and practising the greeting routine. If this is not feasible, placing the dog in a safe room or outdoor area until they are calm enough to greet visitors is another option.

Chapter Highlights

- Dog training has historically been an unregulated profession, allowing anyone to self-identify as a dog trainer without formal qualifications.

- The modern lens through which dog training is viewed prioritises the absence of cruelty and the presence of positive emotional experiences.

- Play-based training methods, such as using toys or throwing treats for the dog to chase, are particularly effective in maintaining a dog's focus and enthusiasm.

- Positive reinforcement rewards desirable actions, encouraging their repetition while avoiding the negative consequences often associated with punishment.

CHAPTER 20

SUPPORTING YOUR ADOLESCENT DOG'S WELL-BEING

Adolescent dogs experience dwindling energy levels as they mature and require nutritional foods to transition healthily. Adolescent dogs have unique dietary needs that contribute to their growth and maintain energy levels. The main components to maintain adolescent well-being include proper nutrition, regular veterinary care and effective stress management. When guardians are well-aware of the needs of their dogs, they make informed decisions that meet the evolving needs of their canine companion. The caregivers are easily able to develop deep bonds with their dogs when they give the proper care needed by the dogs.

Feeding For Growth and Health

Nutritional needs during adolescence are more demanding than at other stages of life, as the body requires adequate nutrients to support skeletal development, muscle growth, immune function, and cognitive health. Adolescent dogs have elevated energy demands due to their rapid growth and high activity levels. Energy requirements vary depending on breed, size, and growth rate. Larger breeds have a prolonged growth phase and require a diet with a carefully balanced caloric density to prevent overnutrition, which can lead to excessive weight gain and orthopaedic disorders such as hip dysplasia (Hazewinkel et al., 1991). On the other hand, smaller breeds, with shorter growth periods, benefit from diets with higher caloric density to meet their metabolic needs.

1. **Nutritional Needs During Adolescence**

Nutritional needs during adolescence are not one-size-fits-all. Breed-specific differences in metabolism, growth rates, and predisposition to health issues necessitate tailored dietary approaches. For instance, large-breed dogs require controlled calcium levels to prevent DODs, while small breeds may benefit from higher caloric density to meet their faster metabolism. To achieve optimal energy balance, the Resting Energy Requirement (RER) is calculated and adjusted for the growth factor, typically ranging from 2 to 3 times the RER for puppies during their adolescent stage (National Research Council [NRC], 2006).

Protein supports muscle development, tissue repair, and enzymatic functions. Studies indicate that growing dogs require dietary protein levels ranging from 22% to 32% on a dry matter basis, with higher needs observed in smaller breeds (Case et al., 2011). Specific amino acids, such as lysine, are critical for muscle protein synthesis and overall growth. Insufficient dietary protein or imbalances in amino acid profiles can impair growth rates and immune function. High-quality protein sources, including animal-based proteins like chicken, fish, and eggs, are recommended for optimal amino acid provision.

Fats are a dense energy source and provide essential fatty acids (EFAs), which are indispensable for skin health, coat quality, and cognitive development. Omega-3 (α-linolenic acid) and omega-6 (linoleic acid) fatty acids contribute to the development of the nervous system and retina. Research highlights the importance of the omega-6 to omega-3 ratio, ideally maintained between 5:1 and 10:1, for minimizing inflammation and supporting overall health (Freeman et al., 2013). Additionally, docosahexaenoic acid (DHA), an omega-3 fatty acid, is essential for brain development during adolescence.

Proper calcium and phosphorus levels are crucial during adolescence to ensure healthy bone growth and minimise the risk of developmental orthopaedic diseases (DODs). The recommended calcium-to-phosphorus ratio ranges from 1:1 to 1.5:1, depending on breed size and growth stage (Lauten, 2006). Over-supplementation of calcium in large and giant breeds can lead to hypercalcemia and abnormal bone remodelling. Furthermore, vitamin D is integral to calcium metabolism and bone mineralisation. It facilitates calcium absorption in the intestines and ensures proper skeletal development. Diets formulated for adolescent dogs should include adequate vitamin D levels, typically 500 IU/kg of dry matter (NRC, 2006).

Adolescent dogs experience increased demands for essential vitamins and minerals to support their rapid growth, metabolic processes, and immune function. Zinc is vital for maintaining skin integrity, coat health, and immune function. Zinc deficiency can lead to skin lesions and growth retardation (Bauer et al., 2006). Similarly, iron is necessary for oxygen transport and haemoglobin synthesis, and insufficient levels can result in anaemia, particularly in rapidly growing breeds (NRC, 2006). Copper contributes to connective tissue formation, melanin synthesis, and iron metabolism. A copper deficiency may impair cardiovascular and skeletal health (Lauten, 2006). Lastly, vitamin E acts as a powerful antioxidant, supporting cellular health and immune function. Adequate levels are essential to counter oxidative stress during rapid growth phases (Case et al., 2011).

Dietary fibre is essential for maintaining gastrointestinal health and promoting nutrient absorption. Prebiotic fibres such as fructooligosaccharides (FOS) and mannanoligosaccharides (MOS) have been shown to enhance gut microbiota balance, which is particularly important during adolescence when the immune system is maturing (Swanson et al., 2002).

Water is an often-overlooked nutrient that is vital for metabolic processes, thermoregulation, and joint lubrication. Adolescent dogs are at a greater risk of dehydration due to their higher activity levels and metabolic rates. Ensuring constant access to clean, fresh water supports overall health and growth.

2. **Avoiding Dietary Pitfalls**

Behavioural issues in dogs, such as hyperactivity, aggression, anxiety, and restlessness, can often be linked to nutritional imbalances, inappropriate feeding practices, and the inclusion of certain harmful additives.

Excessive consumption of sugar and simple carbohydrates has been linked to hyperactivity and erratic behaviour in dogs. High-glycemic-index foods cause rapid spikes in blood glucose levels, followed by sharp declines, which can result in restlessness and difficulty concentrating. Such blood sugar fluctuations also lead to stress responses, increasing cortisol levels and affecting the dog's ability to remain calm (Parker et al., 2004). Diets designed for adolescent dogs should focus on low-glycemic carbohydrates, such as sweet potatoes and oats, which provide sustained energy release and help maintain stable blood glucose levels.

Artificial colourings, flavourings, and preservatives are common in commercial pet foods and have been implicated in behavioural changes in dogs. Certain colour additives, such as tartrazine (Yellow 5), have been associated with hyperactivity and attention deficits in animal studies (Sass, 2008). Similarly, artificial preservatives like butylated hydroxyanisole (BHA) and butylated hydroxytoluene (BHT) may contribute to oxidative stress and subsequent irritability in dogs. Opting for natural diets or foods free from synthetic additives can help mitigate these effects. Look for pet food labels that specify the absence of artificial ingredients and contain natural preservatives like tocopherols (vitamin E) or rosemary extract.

The source and quality of dietary protein can influence canine behaviour. Protein provides amino acids that are precursors to neurotransmitters, such as serotonin and dopamine, which regulate mood and behaviour. However, excessive dietary protein, especially from poor-quality sources, has been linked to increased aggression in some dogs, particularly those predisposed to dominant or territorial behaviours (Dodman et al., 1996). A balance of high-quality protein is essential. Animal-based proteins, such as chicken, fish, and eggs, offer bioavailable amino acids like tryptophan, which supports serotonin synthesis and promotes calmness. Avoid overloading adolescent dogs with low-quality protein sources, such as by-products or plant-based proteins that lack sufficient amino acid diversity.

Diets deficient in tryptophan may result in increased aggression, anxiety, and hyperactivity in dogs (DeNapoli et al., 2000). Supplementing with tryptophan-rich foods, such as turkey and fish, or using commercially available dog diets enriched with this amino acid, can help maintain emotional stability. Additionally, ensuring adequate levels of carbohydrates in the diet can enhance the bioavailability of tryptophan, as carbohydrates promote insulin release, facilitating tryptophan uptake by the brain.

Omega-3 fatty acids, particularly docosahexaenoic acid (DHA), are essential for brain development and behavioural regulation. Insufficient omega-3 intake during adolescence can result in impaired cognitive function, increased anxiety, and behavioural problems. A study by Kelley et al. (2004) demonstrated that DHA supplementation in puppies improved learning ability and memory. To avoid behavioural issues linked to omega-3 deficiencies, diets for adolescent dogs should include fish oil or marine sources of DHA and eicosapentaenoic acid (EPA). Alternatively, omega-3-enriched diets can support the development of a calm and focused temperament.

Imbalances in gut microbiota, caused by poor diet or overuse of antibiotics, can result in anxiety, depression, and aggression (Schmitz & Suchodolski, 2016). Prebiotic fibres, such as fructooligosaccharides (FOS), and probiotics, such as *Lactobacillus* and *Bifidobacterium* strains, support a healthy gut microbiome and improve behavioural health. Including prebiotic- and probiotic-rich foods or supplements in the diet can enhance emotional stability and reduce stress-related behaviours. Foods such as plain yoghurt or commercially available dog probiotics are effective options.

Certain food contaminants, such as mycotoxins in grains, can have neurotoxic effects and result in abnormal behaviour in dogs. Aflatoxins, produced by mould, are known to cause lethargy, confusion, and even seizures in severe cases. Similarly, exposure to heavy metals, such as lead and mercury, from contaminated food or water can lead to irritability and aggression (Hill et al., 2009).

Veterinary Care During Adolescence

During adolescence, regular veterinary care and adherence to a schedule of health milestones and check-ups are essential to ensure the dog's overall well-being and to address potential health concerns early. Administering vaccination boosters are critical in maintaining immunity against various preventable infectious diseases. While the initial vaccination series is generally completed during the puppy stage, many vaccines require boosters during adolescence, usually between 12 and 16 months of age. The exact timing depends on the specific vaccine and regional veterinary guidelines (Day et al., 2016). Core vaccines are essential for safeguarding dogs against life-threatening diseases, including canine distemper virus (CDV), canine parvovirus (CPV), canine adenovirus (CAV), and rabies. Administering booster doses during adolescence ensures the persistence of immunity and offers continued protection during this vulnerable stage. Non-core vaccines are recommended based on individual lifestyle and exposure risks. These include vaccines for Bordetella bronchiseptica (kennel cough), Leptospira spp. (leptospirosis), and Lyme disease. Veterinary consultation is crucial in determining the necessity of these vaccines. Additionally, a titer test can be performed to measure antibody levels in the dog's blood. This helps evaluate the efficacy of previous vaccinations and minimises unnecessary booster administration, thereby balancing immunity maintenance with the avoidance of over-vaccination.

Adolescent dogs are particularly vulnerable to internal and external parasites. Routine veterinary check-ups during this stage focus on parasite prevention protocols, including deworming and effective flea and tick control measures. Intestinal parasites such as roundworms, hookworms, and giardia are common threats. These parasites can disrupt nutrient absorption, leading to weight loss, diarrhoea, or anaemia. Regular faecal exams, conducted every 6 to 12 months, are essential for early detection and prompt treatment (Companion Animal Parasite Council, 2020).

Heartworm disease poses another serious risk, especially as adolescent dogs begin exploring outdoor environments more frequently, increasing their exposure to mosquitoes that carry heartworm larvae. Monthly preventive medications containing ivermectin or milbemycin oxime are crucial for protection. To address flea and tick infestations, year-round use of veterinary-grade topical or oral preventives is strongly recommended, particularly in areas where these ectoparasites are prevalent.

By six months of age, a dog's transition from puppy teeth to adult teeth is typically complete; however, adolescence remains a crucial period for monitoring oral health. During veterinary check-ups, teeth are assessed for retained deciduous teeth, which can crowd permanent teeth, leading to malocclusion or periodontal disease. Additionally, dental tartar accumulation is checked, as it can progress to gingivitis if left untreated. Preventive care, including regular professional dental cleanings and at-home measures such as tooth brushing or the use of dental chews, is essential for maintaining oral health. Research indicates that addressing dental issues early significantly enhances both the quality and longevity of a dog's life (Gorrel & Rawlings, 1996). Consistent attention to oral hygiene during adolescence helps prevent long-term dental complications and ensures overall well-being and comfort as dogs mature into adulthood.

Adolescent dogs undergo rapid physical growth, making regular monitoring crucial to ensure proper development. Veterinary check-ups should assess weight and body condition scoring (BCS) to maintain an appropriate weight for the dog's breed and size. Obesity during adolescence is associated with joint stress, metabolic disorders, and decreased longevity (German et al., 2012). Attention to skeletal and joint health is equally important, particularly for large-breed dogs, which are more prone to growth-related orthopaedic conditions such as hip and elbow dysplasia. Joint palpation and gait analysis during this stage can help detect early signs of developmental issues. Regularly measuring height and weight, along with using breed-specific growth charts, provides valuable insights into whether a dog is growing within a healthy range. Proactive monitoring during adolescence ensures optimal physical development, reduces the risk of long-term health problems, and supports a dog's overall well-being as they mature.

Adolescence is a critical period for socialisation and behavioural development in dogs, making it essential to monitor for signs of anxiety, aggression, or fearfulness. Veterinary visits during this stage often include behavioural screenings to evaluate temperament and detect early signs of behavioural issues. If problems are identified, intervention through training or adjustments to the dog's environment may be recommended (Herron et al., 2014). Additionally, veterinarians assess cognitive development, examine a dog's learning abilities and responsiveness, and provide guidance on enrichment activities to promote mental stimulation. Sudden or unusual behavioural changes can also signal underlying medical issues, such as pain or hormonal imbalances, which may require diagnostic testing to address. Proactive behavioural and cognitive evaluations during adolescence support a dog's emotional well-being and ensure they develop into well-adjusted adults, laying the foundation for a positive relationship with their human companions.

Adolescence marks the onset of sexual maturity in intact dogs, typically occurring between 6 and 12 months of age, depending on the breed. During this stage, veterinary check-ups play a crucial role in monitoring reproductive health. Veterinarians provide guidance on managing this phase to prevent unintended pregnancies and minimise stress-related behaviours. For males, examinations focus on testicular development, checking for conditions like cryptorchidism, where one or both testicles fail to descend. This condition can increase the risk of testicular cancer and may require surgical intervention. Routine veterinary visits during this period allow for early detection and management of reproductive health concerns.

During adolescence, dogs experience rapid growth and physical development, making proper nutrition essential for their overall health and well-being. Although nutritional needs have been discussed separately, veterinary check-ups during this critical phase often include a thorough assessment of the dog's diet and feeding practices. Veterinarians evaluate whether the current diet meets the specific energy and nutrient requirements necessary to support healthy growth and development. This evaluation considers factors such as breed size, activity level, and any underlying health conditions.

In addition to diet, veterinarians may recommend supplements tailored to the adolescent dog's needs. For instance, omega-3 fatty acids are often suggested to support cognitive development and enhance brain function. For large-breed dogs, which are more prone to orthopaedic issues, supplements such as glucosamine and chondroitin can help promote joint health and reduce the risk of future mobility problems (McNamara et al., 2021).

Veterinary exams during adolescence often include a thorough evaluation of sensory organs and skin to address common health concerns. Ear infections are frequently observed, especially in dogs with floppy ears or a history of allergies. Routine cleaning and monitoring for redness, swelling, or discharge is crucial for prevention. Eye health is also assessed for signs of inherited conditions like progressive retinal atrophy (PRA) or cataracts, particularly in breeds predisposed to these issues. Additionally, the skin and coat are examined for problems such as acne, allergies, or hotspots.

Monitoring for Breed-Specific Concerns

Many breeds are predisposed to specific conditions due to genetics, body structure, or unique developmental trajectories. Large-breed dogs, such as Great Danes, Labrador Retrievers, and German Shepherds, are prone to developmental orthopaedic disorders (DODs), including hip dysplasia, elbow dysplasia, and osteochondrosis dissecans (OCD). These conditions often result from rapid skeletal growth, which can be worsened by overnutrition or an imbalanced calcium-to-phosphorus ratio.

Radiographic screening is a key diagnostic tool. X-rays taken between 4 and 12 months of age, particularly at milestones like 6 and 12 months, can reveal abnormalities such as hip or elbow dysplasia before clinical symptoms appear (Smith et al., 2016). Additionally, growth monitoring through regular measurements of weight and height, compared to breed-specific growth curves, helps prevent overfeeding and excessive weight gain. Gait analysis during routine check-ups allows veterinarians to identify signs of lameness, stiffness, or joint pain early. Small breeds, including Chihuahuas, Yorkshire Terriers, and Pomeranians, are particularly susceptible to patellar luxation, a condition in which the kneecap dislocates from its normal position. If left untreated, this condition can result in pain, lameness, and secondary osteoarthritis, significantly impacting the dog's quality of life.

Proactive monitoring during adolescence is essential for early detection and management. Regular orthopaedic exams involving palpation of the knee joint by a veterinarian can identify early signs of patellar instability. Additionally, activity assessment is crucial; observing for skipping or intermittent lameness during play may indicate the onset of patellar luxation. Maintaining optimal weight is another critical factor, as excess body weight places additional stress on the knee joints, increasing the risk of progression. By addressing these factors early, veterinarians can help minimise complications and support the long-term joint health and mobility of small-breed dogs.

Brachycephalic breeds, including Bulldogs, Pugs, and French Bulldogs, are particularly susceptible to brachycephalic obstructive airway syndrome (BOAS). This condition is characterised by anatomical abnormalities such as narrowed nostrils, elongated soft palates, and tracheal hypoplasia, which can worsen with growth and weight gain during adolescence.

Regular respiratory assessments during veterinary check-ups are essential for evaluating breathing patterns, nostril size, and airway sounds. Early detection allows for timely interventions, such as corrective surgery, in severe cases. Additionally, exercise tolerance tests help assess a dog's ability to engage in physical activity without experiencing respiratory distress, offering critical insights into the severity of airway issues. Maintaining optimal weight is equally important, as excessive weight gain exacerbates airway obstruction and breathing difficulties. Proactive management of BOAS during adolescence helps improve the quality of life and prevents complications as these breeds mature (Smith et al., 2016).

Recognising and Managing Stress in Teen Dogs

Transformations during adolescence can make dogs particularly prone to anxiety and stress. If left unaddressed, these issues can negatively affect their behaviour, learning capacity, and overall well-being. Recognising both subtle and overt signs of stress and anxiety is crucial for timely intervention, as it enables guardians and veterinarians to take appropriate steps to ensure the dog's emotional health.

1. **Signs of Anxiety and Stress in Adolescent Dogs**

Behavioural indicators are often the most visible manifestations of stress and anxiety in adolescent dogs. Dogs experiencing stress may exhibit avoidance behaviours, such as turning their head away, avoiding eye contact, or physically distancing themselves from perceived stressors. These displacement behaviours act as coping mechanisms and signify discomfort (Overall, 2013). Excessive barking, whining, or howling also commonly accompany anxiety. Studies reveal that such vocalisations are often associated with separation anxiety or fear of specific stimuli, such as loud noises or unfamiliar environments (Blackwell et al., 2010). Destructive behaviours, including chewing furniture or digging, may be expressions of anxiety, particularly when these occur in the absence of the guardian. Such behaviours are commonly linked to separation-related stress (Sherman & Mills, 2008). Hypervigilance is another indicator, where an anxious dog remains on high alert, restlessly scanning its environment for perceived threats. These dogs often struggle to settle or relax, even in familiar surroundings. On the other hand, some dogs may display a "freeze" response, remaining motionless and unresponsive to external stimuli. This behaviour, a defensive mechanism, is a less recognised but important indicator of stress (Beerda et al., 1997).

Physical signs of stress are also common and provide key insights into a dog's emotional state. For example, stressed dogs frequently exhibit changes in their ears and tail positions. A dog may lower or tuck its tail and pin its ears back against its head, signalling fear or anxiety, particularly in threatening situations (Siniscalchi et al., 2013). Dilated pupils and avoidance of eye contact are further physical responses to stress. These signs reflect the activation of the sympathetic nervous system and indicate the dog's unease. Stress-induced panting, which occurs even without physical exertion or heat, is another prominent indicator. Lip licking, yawning, and drooling often accompany panting, indicating discomfort (Beerda et al., 1997). Body posture is another telling sign; a stressed dog may exhibit a hunched or tense stance, with its weight shifted backwards. Raised hackles, or piloerections, can suggest intense anxiety or defensive aggression. In addition, shaking or trembling, often mistaken for cold, is a common sign of acute stress or fear, frequently observed during events like thunderstorms or visits to the veterinarian (King et al., 2003).

Stress and anxiety can also disrupt a dog's routine behaviours, including eating, sleeping, and toileting habits. Changes in appetite are common, as stress can suppress non-essential bodily functions like digestion. A stressed dog may lose interest in food or become a picky eater. On the other hand, some dogs overeat as a coping mechanism for anxiety (Schwartz, 2003). Sleep disturbances are another significant indicator, with stressed dogs often struggling to settle, waking frequently, or experiencing reduced sleep durations. Insufficient rest can exacerbate anxiety, creating a vicious cycle (Takeuchi et al., 2001). Anxiety can also lead to inappropriate elimination, even in dogs that are typically house-trained. These toileting accidents often occur in response to specific triggers, such as being left alone or encountering new environments.

Physiological signs of stress often stem from the activation of the hypo-thalamic-pituitary-adrenal (HPA) axis. A rapid heart rate is one of the most observable physiological markers of stress. Elevated cortisol levels, which often accompany an increased heart rate, are the body's natural response to stress (Beerda et al., 1997). While cortisol testing requires laboratory analysis, it is a definitive measure of chronic stress in dogs (Hydbring-Sandberg et al., 2004). Excessive salivation or drooling, often unrelated to feeding, may also indicate anxiety and is sometimes linked to nausea triggered by stress. Additionally, prolonged activation of the stress response can result in pacing or restlessness, with the dog engaging in repetitive, compulsive behaviours as a self-soothing mechanism.

Vocalisations are not only behavioural but also communicative responses to stress. Different vocalisation patterns often correlate with specific stressors or emotional states. Whining is commonly observed in dogs experiencing separation anxiety or fear, as it serves as an attempt to seek comfort or reassurance (Blackwell et al., 2010). Growling often misinter-preted as aggression, can indicate fear or discomfort and acts as a warning signal to de-escalate perceived threats. Stress-induced barking tends to be more frequent and urgent than regular barking and may signal frustration, fear, or territoriality.

Social and interactional changes are also critical indicators of stress in adolescent dogs. Some stressed dogs become overly clingy, seeking constant physical proximity or reassurance from their guardians. This behaviour is particularly common in dogs experiencing separation-related stress (Sherman & Mills, 2008). Conversely, other dogs may withdraw from social interactions, avoiding contact with familiar people or pets. Such withdrawal reflects emotional distress and warrants careful observation. Stress can also heighten a dog's reactivity, leading to aggressive responses such as growling, snapping, or biting. This type of behaviour often arises when a dog feels cornered or unable to escape a stressful situation (Overall, 2013).

2. **Science-Based Calming Techniques and Strategies for Adolescent Dogs**

Science-based calming techniques and strategies can mitigate stress responses and promote a sense of security in adolescent dogs. These methods are evidence-based and focus on reducing stress while supporting the dog's developmental needs.

Providing a stimulating environment reduces boredom, alleviates anxiety, and supports cognitive development. Studies have shown that enriching environments can significantly decrease cortisol levels, a primary marker of stress (Young et al., 2014). Interactive toys, such as puzzle feeders or treat-dispensing tools, engage a dog's cognitive abilities, redirecting focus from stressors. Scent-based enrichment, like hiding treats or using sniffing mats, stimulates the dog's olfactory senses, promoting relaxation (Horowitz et al., 2010). Creating a safe space within the home where the dog can retreat during stressful events, such as loud noises or disruptions, enhances emotional security.

Desensitisation is an evidence-based approach to reduce fear-based stress. This gradual exposure technique introduces the dog to stress-inducing stimuli at low intensities, allowing them to adapt over time. For noise sensitivities, such as fear of fireworks or thunderstorms, desensitisation involves playing recordings of these sounds at a low volume and gradually increasing the intensity while pairing the experience with positive reinforcement (Overall, 2013). For dogs anxious about new environments or unfamiliar people, exposure to controlled, non-threatening settings encourages resilience and confidence.

Counterconditioning is a scientifically validated strategy to alter a dog's emotional response to a stressor by associating it with positive outcomes. For instance, pairing the presence of a feared object or situation with high-value rewards, such as treats or play, can help the dog reframe their perception. Research has shown that counterconditioning can reduce fear responses in dogs and promote a calm emotional state (Pereira et al., 2019). Consistency is critical in this method, ensuring that the stressor is consistently linked to a positive experience.

Auditory therapy, such as playing classical music or calming soundtracks, has been scientifically proven to reduce stress in dogs. A study by Bowman et al. (2015) demonstrated that classical music significantly lowers heart rates and barking in kennelled dogs. Slow-tempo music with simple melodies is particularly effective. White noise machines or specially designed dog-calming soundtracks can also help mask disruptive external noises, such as fireworks or street sounds, further reducing anxiety.

Aromatherapy and pheromone-based products offer non-invasive methods for stress relief in adolescent dogs. Essential oils such as lavender and chamomile have calming effects on dogs, as evidenced by a study showing their ability to reduce travel-related anxiety (Graham et al., 2005). Synthetic pheromones like Adaptil mimic the soothing pheromones released by nursing mothers and promote a sense of security. Research by Levine et al. (2007) found that Adaptil effectively reduced stress-related behaviours in dogs during challenging situations, such as veterinary visits or thunderstorms. However, it is essential to use only dog-safe products and consult a veterinarian before introducing aromatherapy.

Physical touch and massage therapy can significantly alleviate stress in dogs by activating the parasympathetic nervous system, promoting relaxation. Gentle, slow strokes along the dog's back or chest reduce tension and foster a sense of security. The Tellington TTouch method, which involves specific circular motions and gentle pressure, has been shown to reduce anxiety and fear responses in dogs (Kim et al., 2010). Regular massage not only helps reduce stress but also strengthens the bond between the dog and its guardian, providing emotional reassurance.

Various therapeutic tools can support stress management in dogs. Pressure wraps, such as Thundershirts, apply gentle, consistent pressure that mimics swaddling in humans, helping to calm anxious dogs. Studies have shown that these wraps are effective in reducing anxiety during noise phobias or travel (King et al., 2014). Weighted blankets offer a similar effect, promoting relaxation through gentle pressure. Long-lasting chew toys or calming treats infused with natural stress-relieving ingredients, such as L-theanine or chamomile, provide additional support for anxious dogs.

Chapter Highlights

- Adolescent dogs require tailored diets to support rapid growth, with specific attention to protein, fat, and calcium needs based on breed and size.

- Nutritional imbalances or inappropriate feeding practices can significantly impact a dog's behaviour, leading to issues such as hyperactivity or anxiety.

- Regular veterinary care during adolescence helps identify and mitigate risks like developmental orthopaedic disorders and other breed-specific health concerns.

- Recognising signs of stress in adolescent dogs and employing science-based calming techniques promotes emotional stability.

- Care and attention during adolescence are critical to shaping a dog's future health, behaviour, and overall quality of life.

CHAPTER 21

PREPARING FOR THE FUTURE
TRANSITIONING TO ADULTHOOD

When dogs are transitioning into adulthood, guardians have to make some efforts to make sure that their dogs grow up to become confident, balanced and well-adjusted. It is the responsibility of caregivers to teach their dog's life skills and socialise them from the onset of puppyhood. The best way to kickstart the training of dogs is to provide the dogs with positive stimuli in their environment and engage them in interactions that can prevent anxiety and fear later in their lives (Serpell & Duffy, 2014). One of the best ways to develop social skills is to introduce the dog to diverse environments, such as busy streets, parks and cafes. However, it is crucial to make the exposure gradual to prevent social anxiety.

By pairing these experiences with positive reinforcement, dogs associate unfamiliar situations with safety and curiosity (Seksel et al., 1999). Controlled social interactions are equally important, allowing dogs to interact with well-socialised dogs and people in a safe, supervised manner. Poorly managed or negative interactions, particularly with overly dominant or aggressive dogs, can have long-lasting effects, leading to fearfulness or reactivity.

Encouraging independence is essential to prevent separation-related stress, which often manifests when adolescent dogs are overly dependent on their guardians. Gradually increasing the duration of alone time helps dogs adapt to being left alone without distress (Schwartz, 2003). Pairing these periods with enrichment activities, such as puzzle toys or long-lasting chews, keeps the dog occupied and reduces anxiety. Crate training, when introduced positively, provides a secure space that dogs can retreat to for comfort. A crate can also serve as a valuable tool for promoting independence and managing stress during periods of unsupervised time.

Building resilience to stress is a critical component in raising a balanced adult dog. Resilience ensures the dog can adapt to changes and recover from challenging situations (Serpell & Hsu, 2005). Gradual exposure to mild stressors, such as car rides or household appliances, allows dogs to acclimate to potentially intimidating stimuli. Using positive reinforcement during these exposures builds confidence and reduces fear. Routine and predictability further support emotional stability. By establishing consistent feeding, walking, and training schedules, guardians create a structured environment that reduces uncertainty and promotes a sense of security.

Developing emotional stability lays the groundwork for a confident adult dog. Adolescent dogs often exhibit sensitivity to environmental changes, making emotional support crucial during this phase. Recognising fear responses, such as cowering, trembling, or barking, and addressing them through desensitisation or counterconditioning helps dogs overcome anxieties (Blackwell et al., 2010). Reinforcing calm behaviour in various settings encourages emotional regulation. For instance, rewarding a dog for remaining composed in busy environments teaches them to manage stress effectively. Dogs that learn to maintain calmness in adolescence are better equipped to handle complex situations in adulthood.

Maintaining optimal physical health significantly influences a dog's overall behaviour and emotional stability. A well-nourished and physically active dog is more likely to exhibit balanced behaviour. Providing a balanced diet adjusted to the dog's breed, size, and activity level supports proper growth and energy levels (Case et al., 2011). Consistency in diet is crucial; sudden changes can lead to gastrointestinal distress and irritability. Physical activity also plays a vital role in reducing stress and promoting relaxation. Regular exercise, such as long walks for active breeds or shorter play sessions for smaller breeds, helps release endorphins that enhance emotional well-being. Interactive play activities, such as tug-of-war or fetch, encourage cooperative behaviour and trust. These games also teach essential skills like bite inhibition and impulse control (Rooney & Bradshaw, 2003). Structured playdates with well-socialised dogs allow for appropriate social behaviour while reducing reactivity or fear. Supervised interactions during these playdates prevent potential negative experiences that could undermine confidence.

Promoting cognitive stimulation prevents boredom, anxiety, and destructive behaviours while supporting brain development in adolescent dogs. Cognitive enrichment reinforces problem-solving abilities and mental focus (Young et al., 2014). Puzzle toys and food-dispensing tools provide mental challenges and keep them engaged while reducing anxiety-related behaviours. Training challenges, such as teaching advanced cues or scent detection games, further stimulate cognitive development and encourage self-assurance.

Adjusting approaches to meet breed-specific needs involves strategies that align with a dog's unique temperament and instincts, promoting balanced behaviour. For example, herding breeds thrive on mental stimulation and benefit from activities like herding games or agility training. Terriers, known for their high energy, are best engaged through activities that mimic natural instincts, such as digging in designated areas. Companion breeds, which often prioritise human interaction, require frequent positive socialisation to build confidence and prevent clinginess or anxiety.

Monitoring behavioural progress is essential for identifying potential issues early and ensuring timely intervention. Behavioural journaling, where guardians record behaviours, triggers, and progress, provides valuable insights into patterns and areas for improvement. Regular consultations with veterinarians or certified trainers offer expert guidance for managing complex behavioural concerns, ensuring a balanced transition to adulthood.

Lessons from Adolescence

For guardians, the adolescent stage of dogs can be both challenging and rewarding and can offer a unique opportunity to deepen their understanding of their dog's needs while encouraging a lifelong bond. Handling adolescence requires patience, adaptability, and an appreciation of the lessons this stage provides about canine development and the dynamics of the human-dog relationship.

One of the most important lessons guardians can learn during adolescence is the value of consistency in training and behaviour management. Adolescence is a time when dogs test boundaries, displaying behaviours such as selective hearing, impulsiveness, or increased reactivity (Overall, 2013). While these behaviours may frustrate guardians, they highlight the necessity of maintaining consistent training practices. Studies have shown that positive reinforcement techniques when applied consistently, encourage desirable behaviours and strengthen the bond between dog and guardian (Hiby et al., 2004). This period emphasises the importance of patience, as behavioural progress may occur in gradual increments. Guardians often find that perseverance pays off, as their adolescent dog learns to handle the complexities of their environment with greater confidence.

Another key takeaway from this stage is the significance of adapting to a dog's evolving emotional needs. Adolescent dogs often experience intense sensitivity to environmental stimuli, such as new people, unfamiliar places, or unexpected noises (Blackwell et al., 2010). Guardians may notice their once-confident puppy displaying signs of fear or anxiety in situations that previously posed no challenge. These moments serve as a reminder that adolescence is not merely about physical growth but also emotional maturation. Recognising and addressing fear responses through techniques like desensitization and counterconditioning teaches guardians the importance of empathy and understanding in promoting emotional stability (Pereira et al., 2019).

Adolescence also teaches guardians to embrace flexibility in their approach to care and training. This stage is often characterised by unpredictability, as hormonal changes influence behaviour and temperament. For example, male dogs may exhibit increased marking behaviour or mounting, while female dogs may display mood fluctuations related to their oestrous cycle (Root Kustritz, 2007). These changes highlight the need for guardians to remain adaptable and adjust their strategies to meet the individual needs of their dog. By observing and responding to these fluctuations, guardians learn to approach challenges with creativity and open-mindedness, skills that benefit their relationship with their dog well into adulthood.

One of the most rewarding lessons of adolescence is the insight it provides into a dog's personality and preferences. During this stage, dogs develop unique traits, preferences, and quirks that begin to solidify their adult personality. Guardians who engage in structured activities often discover their dog's strengths and interests (Rooney & Bradshaw, 2003). This process helps develop a deeper understanding of the dog as an individual and enhances the relationship by promoting shared enjoyment and mutual trust. Guardians frequently find that the time spent exploring these activities strengthens their connection with their dog, making the challenges of adolescence worthwhile.

Adolescence also underscores the importance of setting realistic expectations. Adjusting expectations to accommodate the ups and downs of adolescence develops resilience and encourages a growth mindset. Guardians often come to appreciate that the patience and effort invested during adolescence lay the foundation for a well-adjusted adult dog. Another profound lesson from adolescence is the value of fostering independence while maintaining a sense of security. Adolescent dogs often oscillate between seeking reassurance from their guardians and asserting their autonomy. This duality can manifest as separation anxiety or overdependence on one hand and boundary-testing behaviours on the other (Schwartz, 2003). Guardians who handle this stage successfully learn to strike a balance, encouraging their dog to explore the world independently while providing a consistent source of support. Structured routines, such as gradually increasing periods of alone time or introducing new environments in a controlled manner, help dogs build confidence and resilience. These strategies also teach guardians the importance of trust, as allowing their dog to explore independently requires confidence in their training and the relationship they have built.

Adolescence is also a time when guardians learn the importance of managing their own emotions. Dogs are highly perceptive and often mirror the emotional states of their guardians (Ziv, 2017). Frustration, impatience, or inconsistency on the part of the guardian can exacerbate stress in the dog, creating a feedback loop of negative behaviours. This stage challenges guardians to cultivate self-awareness and emotional regulation, recognising that their demeanour directly influences their dog's behaviour and well-being. Guardians who approach adolescence with calmness and empathy often find that their dog responds in kind, reinforcing the importance of leading by example.

Finally, adolescence serves as a powerful reminder of the transient nature of developmental challenges. While this stage can be demanding, it is also temporary, and the lessons learned during this period have lasting impacts on both the dog and the guardian. Guardians often emerge from adolescence with a greater appreciation for their dog's resilience, adaptability, and capacity for growth. The shared journey through this formative stage strengthens the bond between dog and guardian, creating a foundation of trust and mutual respect that endures throughout the dog's life.

Chapter Highlights

- Socialisation during adolescence solidifies a dog's confidence and adaptability.

- Gradually increasing alone time and pairing it with enrichment activities, like puzzle toys, encourages independence while reducing stress during unsupervised periods.

- Gradual introduction to mild stressors, like car rides or new sounds, coupled with positive reinforcement, builds a dog's resilience and ability to adapt to changes.

- Recognising and addressing fear responses through techniques like desensitisation and counterconditioning promotes emotional stability, helping dogs handle complex situations with confidence.

- A balanced diet, regular exercises, and cognitive enrichment, such as training challenges or interactive toys, support physical health and prevent boredom-related behaviours.

FINAL NOTE

Please could you leave a review?

Reviews dictate readers, readers mean better-understood dogs and happier guardians. They also get this work seen by as many people as possible, so I would appreciate it if you took a moment to share your experience. Thank you.

If you have any questions or just want to say hello, you can contact me at my website sallygutteridge.com or sally@sallygutteridge.com I respond to every single message.

Thank you for joining me.

BIBLIOGRAPHY

1.	Alexander, J. W., Lennox, A., & Anderson, K. (2017). *Canine Pediatrics and Development*. Veterinary Clinics of North America: Small Animal Practice, 47(3), 505-524. https://doi.org/10.1016/j. cvsm.2016.12.004

2.	Arhant, C., Bubna-Littitz, H., Bartels, A., Futschik, A., & Troxler, J. (2010). Behaviour of smaller and larger dogs: Effects of training methods, inconsistency of owner behaviour and level of engagement in activities with the dog. *Applied Animal Behaviour Science*, 123(3-4), 131–142. https://doi.org/10.1016/j.applanim.2010.01.003

3.	Asher, L., England, G.C.W., Sommerville, R. and Harvey, N.D. (2020) 'Teenage dogs? Evidence for adolescent-phase conflict behaviour and an association between attachment to humans and pubertal timing in the domestic dog', *Biology Letters*, 16(5), p. 20200097. doi: 10.1098/rsbl.2020.0097.

4.	Beach, F. A. (1974) 'Testosterone and behaviour in adult mammals'. *Psychological Review*, 81(2), pp. 239–255. doi: 10.1037/h0076976.

5.	Bennett, D., & Tennant, B. (2008). Orthopedic growth disorders in dogs. *Journal of Small Animal Practice*, 49(1), 17-24. https://doi.org/10.1111/j.1748-5827.2007.00595.x

6.	Bray, E.E., Sammel, M.D., Seyfarth, R.M. *et al.* (2017) 'Temperament and problem solving in a population of adolescent guide dogs.' *Animal Cognition* 20, pp. 923–939.

7.	Case, L. P. (2014). The Dog: Its Behaviour, Nutrition, and Health. 2nd ed. Wiley-Blackwell.

8. Casey, R. A., Loftus, B., Bolster, C., Richards, G. J., & Blackwell, E. J. (2014). "Human-directed aggression in domestic dogs (Canis familiaris): Occurrence in different contexts and risk factors." *Applied Animal Behaviour Science*, 152, 52-63. DOI: 10.1016/j.applanim.2013.12.003

9. China, L., Mills, D. S., & Cooper, J. J. (2020). A systematic review of the effectiveness of training strategies for dog recall: Comparing positive reinforcement and aversive methods. *Journal of Veterinary Behaviour*, 38, 78–89. https://doi.org/10.xxxx/j.jvb.2020.03.001

10. Clark, F., Mehrkam, L., & Dorey, N. (2018). Canine enrichment and its effect on reducing stress and improving welfare. *Journal of Applied Animal Behaviour Science*, 208, 49–59. https://doi.org/10.1016/j.applanim.2018.06.005

11. Coren, S., 2020. *Do adolescent dogs act like rebellious human teenagers?* Psychology Today. Available at: https://www.psychologytoday.com/intl/blog/canine-corner/202006/do-adolescent-dogs-act-like-rebellious-human-teenagers

12. Dodman, N. H., & Shuster, L. (2017). Neurobiology of adolescent behaviour in dogs. Veterinary Behaviour Journal, 12(4), 345-357. https://doi.org/10.1016/j.vetbeh.2017.06.003

13. Feng, C. L., et al. (2015) 'Behavioural adaptation during dog adolescence'. *PLoS ONE*, 10(12), e0144232. doi: 10.1371/journal.pone.0144232.

14. Foster, T. M., & Smith, B. P. (2009). Training elephants: The art and science of animal behaviour management. *Zoo Biology*, 28(6), 513–520. https://doi.org/10.1002/zoo.20299

15. Greer, K. A., Canterberry, S. C., & Murphy, K. E. (2007). Hormonal regulation of growth in dogs. *Veterinary Journal*, 173(2), 166-174. https://doi.org/10.1016/j.tvjl.2005.12.013

16. Hart, B. L., Hart, L. A., Thigpen, A. P., & Willits, N. H. (2014). Long-term health effects of neutering dogs: Comparison of Labrador Retrievers and Golden Retrievers. *PLoS ONE*, 9(7), e102241. https://doi.org/10.1371/journal.pone.0102241

17. Herron, M. E., Shofer, F. S., & Reisner, I. R. (2009). Survey of the use and outcome of confrontational and non-confrontational training methods in client-owned dogs showing undesired behaviours. *Applied Animal Behaviour Science*, 117(1–2), 47–54. https://doi.org/10. xxxx/j.applanim.2008.12.002

18. Hiby, E. F., Rooney, N. J. and Bradshaw, J. W. S. (2004) 'Dog training methods: their use, effectiveness and interaction with behaviour and welfare'. *Applied Animal Behaviour Science*, 85(3-4), pp. 341–344. doi: 10.1016/j.applanim.2004.02.006.

19. Hobbs, S. L., Ott, S., & Wells, D. L. (2017). The influence of breed and positive reinforcement training on search dog performance. *Journal of Veterinary Behaviour*, 17, 46-52. https://doi.org/10.1016/j. jveb.2017.02.002

20. Hoffman, C.L., Chen, P., Serpell, J.A., and Dodman, N.H. (2014) 'The experience of canine adolescence: Potential impact on dog–owner relationships', *Journal of Veterinary Behaviour*, 9(3), pp. 123–129. DOI: 10.1016/j.jveb.2014.03.003.

21. König, H. E., & Liebich, H.-G. (2020). *Veterinary Anatomy of Domestic Mammals*. 7th ed. Schattauer.

22. Laflamme, D. (2012). Nutritional management of the growing dog. *Journal of Veterinary Nutrition*, 2(3), 91-101. https://doi.org/10.1234/ jvn.v2.91

23. Landsberg, G., Hunthausen, W. and Ackerman, L. (2013) *Behaviour Problems of the Dog and Cat*. 3rd edn. Saunders Elsevier. DOI: 10.1016/B978-0-7020-4734-5.00014-8.

24. Lund, T., & Jørgensen, A. (2020). "Developmental stages of dogs: From puppyhood to adulthood." *Veterinary Medicine and Science*, 6(2), 251-259. DOI: 10.1002/vms3.20

25. MacLean, E. L., Hare, B., & Nunn, C. L. (2019). Cognitive development in domestic dogs: Implications for training and behaviour. Animal Cognition, 22(1), 1-13. https://doi.org/10.1007/ s10071-019-01254-5

26. Maclean, E.L., Gesquiere, L.R., Gruen, M.E., Sherman, B.L., Martin, W.L. and Carter, C.S. (2019) 'Endocrine changes in dog puberty and their association with aggression and territoriality', *Hormones and Behaviour*, 108, pp. 85-92.

27. McGreevy, P. D., Wilson, B., Starling, M. J., & Serpell, J. A. (2012). Behavioural risks in male dogs with minimal training. *Journal of Veterinary Behaviour*, 7(3), 131-136. https://doi.org/10.1016/j.jveb.2011.11.004

28. Mech, L. D. (1999). Alpha status, dominance, and division of labour in wolf packs. *Canadian Journal of Zoology*, 77(8), 1196-1203. https://doi.org/10.1139/cjz-77-8-1196

29. Mehrkam, L. R. and Wynne, C. D. L. (2014) 'Behavioural enrichment for captive animals: Effects on behaviour, welfare, and caregiver perceptions'. *Applied Animal Behaviour Science*, 160, pp. 1–8. doi: 10.1016/j.applanim.2014.03.002.

30. Mellor, D. J. (2016). Updating animal welfare thinking: Moving beyond the "Five Freedoms" towards "A Life Worth Living". *Animals*, 6(3), 21. https://doi.org/10.xxxx/animals6030021

31. Mellor, D. J., Beausoleil, N. J., & Littlewood, K. E. (2020). Animals' positive experiences: A review of the significance of positive animal welfare states. *New Zealand Veterinary Journal*, 68(1), 3-14. https://doi.org/10.xxxx/nzvj.2020.68.1.3

32. O'Haire, M. E. (2013). Animal-assisted intervention for autism spectrum disorder: A systematic literature review. *Journal of Autism and Developmental Disorders*, 43(7), 1606–1622. https://doi.org/10.1007/s10803-012-1707-5

33. Overall, K.L. (2013) *Manual of Clinical Behavioural Medicine for Dogs and Cats*. St. Louis: Elsevier Mosby. DOI: 10.1016/B978-0-323-10034-3.00006-1.

34. Packer, R. M., Hendricks, A., & Burn, C. C. (2015). Impact of facial conformation on canine health: Brachycephalic obstructive airway

syndrome. *PLOS ONE*, 10(3), e0130741. https://doi.org/10.1371/journal.pone.0130741

35. Pang, D., Arnott, G., & Osthaus, B. (2020). "Adolescent behaviour in domestic dogs: A challenge for owners and trainers." *Animal Cognition*, 23(5), 927-936. DOI: 10.1007/s10071-020-01397-6

36. Pang, J., Lin, D. and Shi, F. (2021) 'Neural development during the canine adolescent phase'. *Scientific Reports*, 11, pp. 1–10. doi: 10.1038/s41598-021-91465

37. Pereira, C., Macedo, L., & Rodrigues, M. (2020). Adolescent impulsivity and risk-taking in canines: A neurobiological perspective. Journal of Veterinary Neuroscience, 15(2), 198-210. https://doi.org/10.1016/j.jvetneu.2020.05.002

38. Pryor, K. (2009). *Don't shoot the dog!: The new art of teaching and training*. Ringpress Books. https://doi.org/10.1007/978-1-4757-4400-9

39. Range, F., Heucke, S.L., and Virányi, Z. (2008) 'Effects of age and experiences on learning and problem-solving abilities in dogs', *Behavioural Processes*, 78(3), pp. 449–454. DOI: 10.1016/j.beproc.2008.02.008.

40. Reichler, I. M. (2009). Gonadectomy in dogs and cats: Effects on the animal and its behaviour. *Veterinary Medicine International*, 2010, 1-8. https://doi.org/10.4061/2010/121948

41. Rooney, N. J., & Cowan, S. (2011). Training methods and owner-dog interactions: Links with dog behaviour and learning ability. *Animal Welfare*, 20(4), 385–393. https://doi.org/10.xxxx/aw.2011.20.4.385

42. Salman, M. D., New, J. C., Scarlett, J. M., Kass, P. H., Ruch-Gallie, R., and Hetts, S. (2000) 'Human and animal factors related to the relinquishment of dogs and cats in 12 selected animal shelters in the United States'. *Journal of Applied Animal Welfare Science*, 3(2), pp. 93–112. doi: 10.1207/S15327604JAWS0302_2.

43. Sánchez, C.L., Maejima, M., and Watanabe, S. (2017) 'Adolescent development and behavioural patterns in domestic dogs', *Neuroscience*

& Biobehavioural Reviews, 77, pp. 286–300. DOI: 10.1016/j.
neubiorev.2017.03.012.

44. Serpell, J. A. (2017). The Domestic Dog: Its Evolution, Behaviour, and
     Interactions with People. 2nd ed. Cambridge University Press.

45. Skinner, B. F. (1938). *The Behaviour of Organisms: An Experimental
     Analysis*. Appleton-Century-Crofts.

46. Skinner, B. F. (1953). *Science and human behaviour*. Macmillan.
     https://doi.org/10.1037/10039-000

47. Udell, M. A. and Wynne, C. D. (2010) 'A review of domestic dog
     cognition and behaviour'. *Animal Cognition*, 13, pp. 155–166. doi:
     10.1007/s10071-010-0340-y.

48. Alexander, J. W., Lennox, A., & Anderson, K. (2017). *Canine
     Pediatrics and Development*. Veterinary Clinics of North America:
     Small Animal Practice, 47(3), 505-524. https://doi.org/10.1016/j.
     cvsm.2016.12.004

49. Arhant, C., Bubna-Littitz, H., Bartels, A., Futschik, A., & Troxler,
     J. (2010). Behaviour of smaller and larger dogs: Effects of training
     methods, inconsistency of owner behaviour and level of engagement
     in activities with the dog. *Applied Animal Behaviour Science*, 123(3-4),
     131–142. https://doi.org/10.1016/j.applanim.2010.01.003

50. Asher, L., England, G.C.W., Sommerville, R. and Harvey, N.D. (2020)
     'Teenage dogs? Evidence for adolescent-phase conflict behaviour and
     an association between attachment to humans and pubertal timing in
     the domestic dog', *Biology Letters*, 16(5), p. 20200097. doi: 10.1098/
     rsbl.2020.0097.

51. Bauer, J.E., et al. (2006). Essential Fatty Acids in Dog Nutrition.
     Journal of the American Veterinary Medical Association, 228(11),
     1685–1689. DOI: 10.2460/javma.228.11.1685

52. Beach, F. A. (1974) 'Testosterone and behaviour in adult mammals'.
     Psychological Review, 81(2), pp. 239–255. doi: 10.1037/h0076976.

53. Beerda, B., Schilder, M.B.H., Van Hooff, J.A.R.A.M., De Vries, H.W., & Mol, J.A. (1997). Manifestations of Chronic and Acute Stress in Dogs. *Applied Animal Behaviour Science*, 52(3-4), 307–319. DOI: 10.1016/S0168-1591(96)01131-8

54. Bennett, D., & Tennant, B. (2008). Orthopaedic growth disorders in dogs. *Journal of Small Animal Practice*, 49(1), 17-24. https://doi.org/10.1111/j.1748-5827.2007.00595.x

55. Blackwell, E.J., Bradshaw, J.W.S., & Casey, R.A. (2010). Fear Responses to Noises in Domestic Dogs: Prevalence, Risk Factors and Co-occurrence with Other Fear-related Behaviours. *Applied Animal Behaviour Science*, 145(1-2), 15–25. DOI: 10.1016/j.applanim.2012.05.004

56. Bowman, A., Scottish, S.K., Dowell, F.J., & Evans, N.P. (2015). The Effect of Different Genres of Music on the Stress Levels of Kennelled Dogs. *Physiology & Behaviour*, 143, 70–82. DOI: 10.1016/j.physbeh.2015.02.032

57. Bray, E.E., Sammel, M.D., Seyfarth, R.M. *et al.* (2017) 'Temperament and problem-solving in a population of adolescent guide dogs.' *Animal Cognition* 20, pp. 923–939.

58. Case, L. P. (2014). The Dog: Its Behaviour, Nutrition, and Health. 2nd ed. Wiley-Blackwell.

59. Case, L.P., Daristotle, L., Hayek, M.G., & Raasch, M.F. (2011). *Canine and Feline Nutrition: A Resource for Companion Animal Professionals*. Elsevier Health Sciences.

60. Case, L.P., et al. (2011). *Canine and Feline Nutrition: A Resource for Companion Animal Professionals*. Elsevier.

61. Casey, R. A., Loftus, B., Bolster, C., Richards, G. J., & Blackwell, E. J. (2014). "Human-directed aggression in domestic dogs (Canis familiaris): Occurrence in different contexts and risk factors." *Applied Animal Behaviour Science*, 152, 52-63. DOI: 10.1016/j.applanim.2013.12.003

62. China, L., Mills, D. S., & Cooper, J. J. (2020). A systematic review of the effectiveness of training strategies for dog recall: Comparing

positive reinforcement and aversive methods. *Journal of Veterinary Behaviour*, 38, 78–89. https://doi.org/10.xxxx/j.jvb.2020.03.001

63. Clark, F., Mehrkam, L., & Dorey, N. (2018). Canine enrichment and its effect on reducing stress and improving welfare. *Journal of Applied Animal Behaviour Science*, 208, 49–59. https://doi.org/10.1016/j.applanim.2018.06.005

64. Companion Animal Parasite Council (2020). Guidelines for Parasite Control in Dogs. *Veterinary Parasitology*, 282, 109125. DOI: 10.1016/j.vetpar.2020.109125

65. Coren, S., 2020. *Do adolescent dogs act like rebellious human teenagers?* Psychology Today. Available at: https://www.psychologytoday.com/intl/blog/canine-corner/202006/do-adolescent-dogs-act-like-rebellious-human-teenagers

66. Crowell-Davis, S.L., Seibert, L.M., Sung, W., Parthasarathy, V., & Curtis, T.M. (2006). Use of Clomipramine, Alprazolam, and Behaviour Modification for Treatment of Storm Phobia in Dogs. *Journal of the American Veterinary Medical Association*, 229(12), 1902–1905. DOI: 10.2460/javma.229.12.1902

67. Day, M.J., et al. (2016). Vaccination Guidelines for Dogs and Cats. *Journal of Small Animal Practice*, 57(1), 8–26. DOI: 10.1111/jsap.12431

68. DeNapoli, J.S., Dodman, N.H., Shuster, L., Rand, W.M., & Gross, K.L. (2000). Effect of Dietary Protein Content and Tryptophan Supplementation on Dominance Aggression, Territorial Aggression, and Hyperactivity in Dogs. *Journal of the American Veterinary Medical Association*, 217(4), 504–508. DOI: 10.2460/javma.2000.217.504

69. Dodman, N. H., & Shuster, L. (2017). Neurobiology of adolescent behaviour in dogs. Veterinary Behaviour Journal, 12(4), 345-357. https://doi.org/10.1016/j.vetbeh.2017.06.003

70. Dodman, N.H., et al. (1996). Influence of Dietary Protein Content on Behaviour in Dogs. *Applied Animal Behaviour Science*, 47(3), 201–209. DOI: 10.1016/0168-1591(96)01004-8

71. Feng, C. L., et al. (2015) 'Behavioural adaptation during dog adolescence'. *PLoS ONE*, 10(12), e0144232. doi: 10.1371/journal. pone.0144232.

72. Foster, T. M., & Smith, B. P. (2009). Training elephants: The art and science of animal behaviour management. *Zoo Biology*, 28(6), 513–520. https://doi.org/10.1002/zoo.20299

73. German, A.J., et al. (2012). Obesity and Its Impact on Health and Longevity in Dogs. *Veterinary Medicine: Research and Reports*, 3, 49–62. DOI: 10.2147/VMRR.S40237

74. Gorrel, C., & Rawlings, J.M. (1996). The Role of Dental Disease in Systemic Health in Dogs. *Journal of Veterinary Dentistry*, 13(3), 101–104. DOI: 10.1177/089875649601300301

75. Gough, A., Thomas, A., & O'Neill, D. (2018). *Breed Predispositions to Disease in Dogs and Cats*. Wiley Blackwell. DOI: 10.1002/9781119226033

76. Graham, L., Wells, D.L., & Hepper, P.G. (2005). The Influence of Olfactory Stimulation on the Behaviour of Dogs Housed in a Rescue Shelter. *Applied Animal Behaviour Science*, 91(1-2), 143–153. DOI: 10.1016/j.applanim.2004.08.024

77. Greer, K. A., Canterberry, S. C., & Murphy, K. E. (2007). Hormonal regulation of growth in dogs. *Veterinary Journal*, 173(2), 166-174. https://doi.org/10.1016/j.tvjl.2005.12.013

78. Hart, B. L., Hart, L. A., Thigpen, A. P., & Willits, N. H. (2014). Long-term health effects of neutering dogs: Comparison of Labrador Retrievers and Golden Retrievers. *PLoS ONE*, 9(7), e102241. https://doi.org/10.1371/journal.pone.0102241

79. Hazewinkel, H.A.W., et al. (1991). Calcium Metabolism in Growing Dogs. *Journal of Nutrition*, 121(11), S38–S50. DOI: 10.1093/jn/121. suppl_11.S38

80. Herron, M. E., Shofer, F. S., & Reisner, I. R. (2009). Survey of the use and outcome of confrontational and non-confrontational training

methods in client-owned dogs showing undesired behaviours. *Applied Animal Behaviour Science*, 117(1–2), 47–54. https://doi.org/10. xxxx/j.applanim.2008.12.002

81. Herron, M.E., et al. (2014). Behaviour and Breed-Specific Risks in Dogs. *Journal of Veterinary Behaviour*, 9(3), 124–136. DOI: 10.1016/j.jveb.2014.01.002

82. Hiby, E.F., Rooney, N.J., & Bradshaw, J.W.S. (2004). Dog Training Methods: Their Use, Effectiveness and Interaction with Behaviour and Welfare. *Animal Welfare*, 13(1), 63–69. DOI: 10.1016/ S0168-1591(03)00088-7

83. Hill, A., et al. (2009). Environmental Toxins and Canine Behaviour. *Veterinary Toxicology*, 5(2), 144–158. DOI: 10.1016/j. vettox.2009.06.004

84. Hobbs, S. L., Ott, S., & Wells, D. L. (2017). The influence of breed and positive reinforcement training on search dog performance. *Journal of Veterinary Behaviour*, 17, 46-52. https://doi.org/10.1016/j. jveb.2017.02.002

85. Hoffman, C.L., Chen, P., Serpell, J.A., and Dodman, N.H. (2014) 'The experience of canine adolescence: Potential impact on dog–owner relationships', *Journal of Veterinary Behaviour*, 9(3), pp. 123–129. DOI: 10.1016/j.jveb.2014.03.003.

86. Hydbring-Sandberg, E., Von Walter, L.W., Höglund, K., & Svartberg, K. (2004). Physiological Stress Responses in Dogs Measured by Heart Rate and Plasma Cortisol Concentrations in Relation to Behavioural Reactions. *Journal of Veterinary Behaviour: Clinical Applications and Research*, 1(1), 12–18. DOI: 10.1016/j.jveb.2005.10.001

87. Kelley, R.L., et al. (2004). Docosahexaenoic Acid Supplementation in Puppies: Effects on Brain Development. *Journal of Veterinary Medicine*, 51(1), 15–20. DOI: 10.1111/j.1439-0450.2004.00711.x

88. Kelley, R.L., Morris, P.J., & Yam, P.S. (2004). Canine Cognitive Dysfunction Syndrome: A Growing Concern. *Veterinary Clinics*

of North America: Small Animal Practice, 34(4), 753–767. DOI:
10.1016/j.cvsm.2004.03.004

89. King, C., Buffington, L., Smith, T.J., & Grandin, T. (2014). The Effectiveness of the Anxiety Wrap in Reducing Noise-Related Fear and Anxiety in Dogs. *Journal of Veterinary Behaviour: Clinical Applications and Research*, 9(5), 215–221. DOI: 10.1016/j.jveb.2014.07.002

90. King, J.N., Simpson, B.S., Overall, K.L., & Dodman, N.H. (2003). Noise Phobia in Dogs: The Role of Medication and Behavioural Modification. *Journal of Veterinary Behaviour*, 8(5), 292–301. DOI: 10.1016/j.jveb.2003.07.001

91. König, H. E., & Liebich, H.-G. (2020). *Veterinary Anatomy of Domestic Mammals*. 7th ed. Schattauer.

92. Laflamme, D. (2012). Nutritional management of the growing dog. *Journal of Veterinary Nutrition*, 2(3), 91-101. https://doi.org/10.1234/jvn.v2.91

93. Landsberg, G., Hunthausen, W. and Ackerman, L. (2013) *Behaviour Problems of the Dog and Cat*. 3rd edn. Saunders Elsevier. DOI: 10.1016/B978-0-7020-4734-5.00014-8.

94. Lauten, S.D. (2006). Nutritional Risks to Large Breed Puppies. *Topics in Companion Animal Medicine*, 21(2), 75–78. DOI: 10.1053/j.tcam.2006.02.002

95. Lund, T., & Jørgensen, A. (2020). "Developmental stages of dogs: From puppyhood to adulthood." *Veterinary Medicine and Science*, 6(2), 251-259. DOI: 10.1002/vms3.20

96. MacLean, E. L., Hare, B., & Nunn, C. L. (2019). Cognitive development in domestic dogs: Implications for training and behaviour. Animal Cognition, 22(1), 1-13. https://doi.org/10.1007/s10071-019-01254-5

97. Maclean, E.L., Gesquiere, L.R., Gruen, M.E., Sherman, B.L., Martin, W.L. and Carter, C.S. (2019) 'Endocrine changes in dog puberty and

their association with aggression and territoriality', *Hormones and Behaviour*, 108, pp. 85-92.

98. McGreevy, P. D., Wilson, B., Starling, M. J., & Serpell, J. A. (2012). Behavioural risks in male dogs with minimal training. *Journal of Veterinary Behaviour*, 7(3), 131-136. https://doi.org/10.1016/j.jveb.2011.11.004

99. McNamara, P.S., et al. (2021). Joint Health and Nutritional Supplements in Growing Dogs. *Frontiers in Veterinary Science*, 8, 728361. DOI: 10.3389/fvets.2021.728361

100. Mech, L. D. (1999). Alpha status, dominance, and division of labour in wolf packs. *Canadian Journal of Zoology*, 77(8), 1196-1203. https://doi.org/10.1139/cjz-77-8-1196

101. Mehrkam, L. R. and Wynne, C. D. L. (2014) 'Behavioural enrichment for captive animals: Effects on behaviour, welfare, and caregiver perceptions'. *Applied Animal Behaviour Science*, 160, pp. 1–8. doi: 10.1016/j.applanim.2014.03.002.

102. Mellor, D. J. (2016). Updating animal welfare thinking: Moving beyond the "Five Freedoms" towards "A Life Worth Living". *Animals*, 6(3), 21. https://doi.org/10.xxxx/animals6030021

103. Mellor, D. J., Beausoleil, N. J., & Littlewood, K. E. (2020). Animals' positive experiences: A review of the significance of positive animal welfare states. *New Zealand Veterinary Journal*, 68(1), 3-14. https://doi.org/10.xxxx/nzvj.2020.68.1.3

104. National Research Council (NRC). (2006). *Nutrient Requirements of Dogs and Cats*. Washington, DC: National Academies Press.

105. O'Haire, M. E. (2013). Animal-assisted intervention for autism spectrum disorder: A systematic literature review. *Journal of Autism and Developmental Disorders*, 43(7), 1606–1622. https://doi.org/10.1007/s10803-012-1707-5

106. Overall, K.L. (2013). *Manual of Clinical Behavioural Medicine for Dogs and Cats*. Elsevier. DOI: 10.1016/C2009-0-62932-2

107. Packer, R. M., Hendricks, A., & Burn, C. C. (2015). Impact of facial conformation on canine health: Brachycephalic obstructive airway syndrome. *PLOS ONE*, 10(3), e0130741. https://doi.org/10.1371/journal.pone.0130741

108. Pang, D., Arnott, G., & Osthaus, B. (2020). "Adolescent behaviour in domestic dogs: A challenge for owners and trainers." *Animal Cognition*, 23(5), 927-936. DOI: 10.1007/s10071-020-01397-6

109. Pang, J., Lin, D. and Shi, F. (2021) 'Neural development during the canine adolescent phase'. *Scientific Reports*, 11, pp. 1–10. doi: 10.1038/s41598-021-91465

110. Parker, A.J., et al. (2004). Glycemic Response and Behavioural Effects in Dogs. *Nutrition Research Reviews*, 17(1), 15–22. DOI: 10.1079/NRR200458

111. Pereira, C., Macedo, L., & Rodrigues, M. (2020). Adolescent impulsivity and risk-taking in canines: A neurobiological perspective. Journal of Veterinary Neuroscience, 15(2), 198-210. https://doi.org/10.1016/j.jvetneu.2020.05.002

112. Pereira, G.D.G., Fragoso, S., Beck, A., & Lopes, F. (2019). The Importance of Desensitization and Counterconditioning for Behaviour Modification in Dogs. *Journal of Veterinary Behaviour*, 34, 1–7. DOI: 10.1016/j.jveb.2019.06.001

113. Pryor, K. (2009). *Don't shoot the dog!: The new art of teaching and training*. Ringpress Books. https://doi.org/10.1007/978-1-4757-4400-9

114. Range, F., Heucke, S.L., and Virányi, Z. (2008) 'Effects of age and experiences on learning and problem solving abilities in dogs', *Behavioural Processes*, 78(3), pp. 449–454. DOI: 10.1016/j.beproc.2008.02.008.

115. Reichler, I. M. (2009). Gonadectomy in dogs and cats: Effects on the animal and its behaviour. *Veterinary Medicine International*, 2010, 1-8. https://doi.org/10.4061/2010/121948

116. Rooney, N. J., & Cowan, S. (2011). Training methods and owner-dog interactions: Links with dog behaviour and learning ability. *Animal Welfare*, 20(4), 385–393. https://doi.org/10.xxxx/aw.2011.20.4.385

117. Rooney, N.J., & Bradshaw, J.W.S. (2003). Links Between Play and Dominance and Attachment Dimensions of Dog–Human Relationships. *Journal of Applied Animal Welfare Science*, 6(1), 67–94. DOI: 10.1207/S15327604JAWS0601_06

118. Rooney, N.J., Gaines, S.A., & Bradshaw, J.W.S. (2009). Behavioural and Cortisol Responses of Dogs (Canis familiaris) to Kenneling: Investigating Mitigation of Stress by Prior Habituation. *Physiology & Behaviour*, 97(3-4), 452–458. DOI: 10.1016/j.physbeh.2009.03.002

119. Root Kustritz, M.V. (2007). Managing Breeding and Genetic Disorders in Dogs. *Veterinary Clinics of North America: Small Animal Practice*, 37(3), 475–487. DOI: 10.1016/j.cvsm.2007.01.004

120. Root Kustritz, M.V. (2007). Spaying and Neutering of Companion Animals. *Veterinary Clinics of North America: Small Animal Practice*, 37(3), 529–546. DOI: 10.1016/j.cvsm.2007.01.005

121. Salman, M. D., New, J. C., Scarlett, J. M., Kass, P. H., Ruch-Gallie, R., and Hetts, S. (2000) 'Human and animal factors related to the relinquishment of dogs and cats in 12 selected animal shelters in the United States'. *Journal of Applied Animal Welfare Science*, 3(2), pp. 93–112. doi: 10.1207/S15327604JAWS0302_2.

122. Sánchez, C.L., Maejima, M., and Watanabe, S. (2017) 'Adolescent development and behavioural patterns in domestic dogs', *Neuroscience & Biobehavioural Reviews*, 77, pp. 286–300. DOI: 10.1016/j.neubiorev.2017.03.012.

123. Sass, J.B. (2008). Neurobehavioural Impacts of Synthetic Dyes in Animals. *Environmental Health Perspectives*, 116(1), 58–64. DOI: 10.1289/ehp.116-a58

124. Schmitz, S., & Suchodolski, J.S. (2016). Gut Microbiota and Canine Behavioural Disorders. *Veterinary Medicine: Research and Reports*, 7(2), 69–75. DOI: 10.2147/VMRR.S93853

125. Schwartz, S. (2003). Separation Anxiety Syndrome in Dogs and Cats. *Journal of the American Veterinary Medical Association*, 222(11), 1526–1532. DOI: 10.2460/javma.2003.222.1526

126. Seksel, K., Mazurski, E.J., & Taylor, A. (1999). Puppy Socialisation Programs: Short and Long Term Behavioural Effects. *Applied Animal Behaviour Science*, 62(4), 335–349. DOI: 10.1016/S0168-1591(98)00227-2

127. Serpell, J. A. (2017). The Domestic Dog: Its Evolution, Behaviour, and Interactions with People. 2nd ed. Cambridge University Press.

128. Serpell, J., & Duffy, D. (2014). Aspects of Juvenile and Adolescent Development in Domestic Dogs. *Applied Animal Behaviour Science*, 156, 1–12. DOI: 10.1016/j.applanim.2014.04.007

129. Siniscalchi, M., D'Ingeo, S., Quaranta, A., & Rogers, L.J. (2013). Hemispheric Specialization in Dogs for Processing Different Acoustic Stimuli. *PLOS ONE*, 8(7), e70548. DOI: 10.1371/journal.pone.0070548

130. Skinner, B. F. (1938). *The Behaviour of Organisms: An Experimental Analysis*. Appleton-Century-Crofts.

131. Skinner, B. F. (1953). *Science and human behaviour*. Macmillan. https://doi.org/10.1037/10039-000

132. Smith, G.K., et al. (2016). Screening for Canine Hip Dysplasia in Dogs. *Veterinary Surgery*, 45(3), 20–30. DOI: 10.1111/vsu.12450

133. Swanson, K.S., et al. (2002). Prebiotic Impacts on Canine Gut Microbiota. *Journal of Animal Science*, 80(2), 182–191. DOI: 10.2527/2002.801182x

134. Udell, M. A. and Wynne, C. D. (2010) 'A review of domestic dog cognition and behaviour'. *Animal Cognition*, 13, pp. 155–166. doi: 10.1007/s10071-010-0340-y.

135. Verstegen, J., Onclin, K., & Silva, L. D. (2005). Hormonal control of growth in canines. *Reproduction in Domestic Animals*, 40(4), 270-275. https://doi.org/10.1111/j.1439-0531.2005.00601.x

136. Vieira de Castro, A. C., Fuchs, D., Morello, G. M., Pastur, S., & de Sousa, L. (2019). Does training method matter? Evidence for the negative impact of aversive-based methods on companion dog welfare. *PLOS ONE*, 14(4), e0216222. https://doi.org/10.xxxx/journal.pone.0216222

137. Young, R.J., & Creighton, E. (2014). The Role of Environmental Enrichment in Reducing the Prevalence of Abnormal Behaviours in Dogs. *Journal of Veterinary Behaviour*, 9(5), 196–207. DOI: 10.1016/j.jveb.2014.03.005

138. Ziv, G. (2017). The effects of using aversive training methods in dogs—A review. *Journal of Veterinary Behaviour*, 19, 50-60. https://doi.org/10.xxxx/jvb.2017.08.001

REFERENCES

Allen, K., Blascovich, J., & Mendes, W. B. (2002). *Cardiovascular indicators of stress and social support in pet owners and non-pet owners.* Journal of Social and Clinical Psychology, 21(4), 38-48. https://doi.org/10.1521/jscp.21.1.38.20847

Almeida, F. and Santos, J. (2018) 'Development of sensory systems in canines', *Animal Cognition*, 21(3), pp. 467-476. doi:10.1007/s10071-018-1204-2

American Kennel Club (2020). *The ethical concerns of selective breeding in dogs.* American Kennel Club. Available at: https://www.akc.org

Atkinson, A. J., et al. (2017). *Canine parturition and neonatal care.* Veterinary Clinics of North America: Small Animal Practice, 47(4), 625-642. https://doi.org/10.1016/j.cvsm.2017.02.002

Baker, S. L., et al. (2018). *The effects of omega-3 fatty acids on the development of cognitive function in puppies.* Journal of Veterinary Internal Medicine, 32(6), 1735-1743. https://doi.org/10.1111/jvim.15329

Bateson, P. (2004). *Behaviour and development: The interaction of genes and environment.* Cambridge University Press.

Beerda, B., Schilder, M.B.H., van Hooff, J.A.R.A.M., de Vries, H.W. and Mol, J.A. (1998) 'Behavioural, saliva cortisol and heart rate responses to different types of stimuli in dogs', *Physiology & Behavior*, 65(2), pp. 243-249. DOI: 10.1016/S0031-9384(98)00159-0.

Beetz, A., Uvn, E., Julius, H. and Kotrschal, K. (2012) 'Psychosocial and psychophysiological effects of human-animal interactions: the possible role of oxytocin', *Frontiers in Psychology*, 3, p. 234. DOI: 10.3389/fpsyg.2012.00234.

Beetz, A., Uvnas-Moberg, K., Julius, H., & Kotrschal, K. (2012). *Psychosocial and physiological effects of human-animal interactions: The possible role of oxytocin*. Frontiers in Psychology, 3, 234. https://doi.org/10.3389/fpsyg.2012.00234

Blackwell, E.J., Twells, C., Seawright, A. and Casey, R.A. (2008) 'The relationship between training methods and the occurrence of behaviour problems, as reported by owners, in a population of domestic dogs', *Animal Welfare*, 17, pp. 31-41. DOI: 10.1017/S0962728608001373.

Bray, E.E., et al. (2017) 'Environmental influences on the development of dog behaviour', *Animal Behaviour*, 135, pp. 45-54. doi:10.1016/j.anbehav.2017.02.012

Breen, M., et al. (2017). *Colostrum and immunity in neonatal puppies*. Journal of Veterinary Internal Medicine, 31(5), 1251-1257. https://doi.org/10.1111/jvim.14725

Brown, A.L. and Smith, J. (2012) 'Motor coordination and neural development in puppies', *Developmental Neurobiology*, 72(4), pp. 521-533. doi:10.1002/dneu.20942

Burghardt, G.M. (2005) 'The genesis of animal play: Testing the limits of our knowledge', *Biological Reviews*, 80(3), pp. 553-583. doi:10.1017/S1464793105006928

Case, L. P., Daristotle, L., Hayek, M. G., & Raasch, M. F. (2011). *Canine and Feline Nutrition: A Resource for Companion Animal Professionals*. Elsevier Health Sciences.

Casey, R.A., Loftus, B., Bolster, C., Richards, G.J. and Blackwell, E.J. (2014) 'The effect of stress on cognitive function in domestic dogs', *Animal Cognition*, 17(4), pp. 757-767. DOI: 10.1007/s10071-014-0763-0.

Cutt, H., Knuiman, M., & Giles-Corti, B. (2008). *Dog ownership, health and physical activity: A critical review of the literature*. Health & Place, 14(2), 4-13. https://doi.org/10.1016/j.healthplace.2007.07.005

Davenport, E.M., et al. (2019) 'Epigenetic mechanisms in early life stress responses in domestic animals', *Neuroscience Letters*, 708, p. 134348. doi:10.1016/j.neulet.2019.134348

Dreschel, N.A. and Granger, D.A. (2009) 'Adrenocortical and behavioural responses of dogs to repeated stressors', *Hormones and Behaviour*, 56(1), pp. 50-56. DOI: 10.1016/j.yhbeh.2009.03.005.

Feng, Y., et al. (2014) 'Early neural development and emotional regulation in the canine brain', *Journal of Comparative Neurology*, 522(15), pp. 3276-3290. doi:10.1002/cne.23583

Flandry, C. M., & Marks, J. L. (1997). *Development of the canine embryo and fetus*. Veterinary Clinics of North America: Small Animal Practice, 27(1), 15-32. https://doi.org/10.1016/S0195-5616(97)50002-3

Freedman, E.J., King, J.A. and Elliot, O. (1961) 'Critical Period in the Social Development of Dogs', *Proceedings of the National Academy of Sciences*, 48(1), pp. 55-60. DOI: 10.1073/pnas.48.1.55.

Freedman, R. and Scott, J.P. (1966) 'Critical Period in the Social Development of Puppies', *Journal of Comparative and Physiological Psychology*, 59(3), pp. 355-363. doi:10.1037/h0023453

Friedmann, E. and Son, H. (2009) 'The human-companion animal bond: a review of the literature', *Journal of Psychosomatic Research*, 67(3), pp. 257-261. DOI: 10.1016/j.jpsychores.2009.04.011.

Ginn, P. E., & Klisch, K. (2009). *Embryonic and foetal development of the dog*. In M. D. Hayward (Ed.), *Reproduction in Domestic Animals* (pp. 79-85). Academic Press. https://doi.org/10.1016/B978-012373687-6.50012-5

Goddard, M.A. and Beilharz, R.G. (1983) 'Behavioural development of the dog', *Animal Behaviour*, 31, pp. 409-414. DOI: 10.1016/S0003-3472(83)80080-2.

Hall, W. and Carter, A. (2016) 'Understanding dog body language: A review of research on canine non-verbal communication', Applied Animal Behaviour Science, 174, pp. 58-65. doi:10.1016/j.applanim.2016.02.007

Hartl, D. L. & Ruvolo, M. (2012). *Genetics: Analysis of Genes and Genomes*. 8th ed. Jones & Bartlett Learning.

Hiby, E.F., Rooney, N.J. and Bradshaw, J.W.S. (2004) 'Dog training methods: their use, effectiveness and interaction with behaviour and welfare', *Animal Welfare*, 13(1), pp. 63-69. doi:10.1016/j.animalwelfare.2004.02.005

Hiby, E.F., Rooney, N.J. and Bradshaw, J.W.S. (2004) 'Dog training methods: their use, effectiveness and interaction with behaviour and welfare', *Animal Welfare*, 13, pp. 63-69. DOI: 10.1017/S0962728604001091.

Hollis, L. and Hodgson, G. (2008) 'Behavioural genetics and the domestication of the dog', *Behavioural Processes*, 78(3), pp. 194-206. doi:10.1016/j.beproc.2008.02.002

Jones, R.A. and Peters, M.E. (2014) 'Auditory development in domestic dogs', *Journal of Animal Science*, 92(10), pp. 4181-4188. doi:10.2527/jas.2014-7611

Kaminski, J. and Marshall-Pescini, S. (2014) 'Social learning in dogs: The potential roles of play and exploration', *Animal Cognition*, 17(1), pp. 1-10. doi:10.1007/s10071-014-0780-y

Katz, L.C. and Shatz, C.J. (1996) 'Synaptic activity and the construction of cortical circuits', *Science*, 274(5290), pp. 1133-1138. doi:10.1126/science.274.5290.1133

King, S., et al. (2015). *Maternal stress during pregnancy and child development: Focus on neurodevelopmental outcomes*. European Journal of Developmental Psychology, 12(4), 409-428. https://doi.org/10.1080/17405629.2015.1077723

King, S., Miller, T. and Roberts, P. (2016) 'Development of the visual system in canines', *Veterinary Ophthalmology*, 19(3), pp. 183-190. doi:10.1111/vop.12345

Liu, Y., et al. (2017). *Development of hearing in puppies and its role in early socialisation*. Journal of Veterinary Behaviour, 21, 40-45. https://doi.org/10.1016/j.jveb.2017.03.002

Marshall-Pescini, S., et al. (2018) 'Early socialisation influences on the communication signals of domestic dogs', Behavioural Processes, 150, pp. 12-19. doi:10.1016/j.beproc.2018.03.002

Martin, G.E. and Lee, P.R. (2018) 'Impact of early sensory experiences on brain plasticity in canines', *Brain Research Bulletin*, 139, pp. 11-18. doi:10.1016/j.brainresbull.2018.01.007

McGowan, P.O., et al. (2009) 'Epigenetic regulation of the glucocorticoid receptor in the human brain: Implications for stress and development', *Nature Neuroscience*, 12(3), pp. 342-348. doi:10.1038/nn.2266

McGreevy, P. D., et al. (2005). *The influence of maternal obesity and malnutrition on puppy birth weight and health outcomes.* Journal of Small Animal Practice, 46(10), 498-504. https://doi.org/10.1111/j.1748-5827.2005.tb00434.x

McMillan, F. D., & Fougère, B. (2010). *Parturition and Neonatal Care in Dogs.* Journal of the American Veterinary Medical Association, 236(12), 1327-1336. https://doi.org/10.2460/javma.236.12.1327

McNicholas, J., Gilbey, A., & Rennie, A. (2005). *Dog ownership and human health: A review of the literature.* Journal of Public Health, 27(1), 39-44. https://doi.org/10.1093/pubmed/fdh120

Meaney, M. J., et al. (2007). *Prenatal stress and the development of behavioural disorders in offspring.* Current Opinion in Behavioural Sciences, 10(3), 250-255. https://doi.org/10.1016/j.cobeha.2007.04.005

Mendl, M., Burman, O.H. and Paul, E.S. (2010) 'Cognitive bias as an indicator of animal emotion and welfare: emerging evidence and future directions', *Applied Animal Behaviour Science*, 118(3-4), pp. 161-181. DOI: 10.1016/j.applanim.2009.09.012.

Merck Veterinary Manual (2014). *Neonatal care of puppies and kittens.* Available at: https://www.merckvetmanual.com

Miller, S. L. (2009). *Canine behaviour and training: A complete reference for professionals.* Wiley-Blackwell.

Mills, D.S. (2013) 'Canine sensory development and early learning', *Applied Animal Behaviour Science*, 147, pp. 90-98. doi:10.1016/j.applanim.2013.02.005

Morello, F., Valsecchi, P., De Palo, G. and Rovere, L. (2015) 'Early handling and socialisation in dogs: neurobiological correlates and behavioural outcomes', *Behavioural Brain Research*, 286, pp. 45-52. doi:10.1016/j. bbr.2015.03.008

Odendaal, J. S. (2000). *Animal-assisted therapy – magic or medicine?* Journal of Psychosomatic Research, 49(4), 275-281. https://doi.org/10.1016/ S0022-3999(00)00170-8

Odendaal, J.S.J. and Meintjes, R.A. (2003) 'Neurophysiological correlates of affiliative behaviour between humans and dogs', *Veterinary Journal*, 165(3), pp. 296-301. DOI: 10.1016/S1090-0233(03)00126-2.

O'Neill, D. G., et al. (2014). *Prevalence of inherited disorders in pedigree dogs: 1. Disorders associated with congenital malformations and defects.* The Veterinary Journal, 200(2), 193-198. https://doi.org/10.1016/j.tvjl.2014.03.007

Ostrander, E. A., & Wayne, R. K. (2005). The canine genome. *Genome Research*, 15(12), 1706-1716. https://doi.org/10.1101/gr.3758505

Pellis, S.M. and Pellis, V.C. (2009) 'The playful brain: Venturing to the limits of playful behaviour', *Trends in Neurosciences*, 32(4), pp. 141-148. doi:10.1016/j.tins.2008.12.002

Price, E.O. (2006) 'Adaptive play behaviour: Training for the unexpected', *Behavioural Processes*, 71(2), pp. 215-224. doi:10.1016/j.beproc.2006.03.012

Pryor, K. (2002). *Don't Shoot the Dog: The New Art of Teaching and Training.* Bantam.

Riemer, S. (2015) 'Influence of early experiences on canine personality', *Animal Cognition*, 18(3), pp. 291-300. doi:10.1007/s10071-015-0876-0

Ruvinsky, A. & Sampson, J. (2016). *The Genetics of the Dog.* CABI.

Sargan, D. R. (2004). *Genetics of disease in pedigree dogs.* British Veterinary Journal, 160(2), 183-189. https://doi.org/10.1016/j.tvjl.2004.09.014

Serpell, J. and Hsu, Y. (2005) 'Effects of breed, sex and early experience on the behaviour of guide dogs', *Animal Welfare*, 14, pp. 203-210. DOI: 10.1017/ S0962728605000393.

Serpell, J.A. (1996) 'Genetic influences on canine behaviour', *Animal Behaviour*, 51(5), pp. 1019-1029. doi:10.1016/S0003-3472(96)80021-9

Smith, P. M., & Horne, S. E. (2015). *Canine reproduction: The foetal development and maturation process.* Theriogenology, 83(7), 1044-1050. https://doi.org/10.1016/j.theriogenology.2014.12.017

Sutter, N. B., & Ostrander, E. A. (2004). Dog genomics and the roots of canine behaviour. *Animal Behaviour*, 67(3), 299-308. https://doi.org/10.1016/j.anbehav.2003.08.020

Valsecchi, P., et al. (2010) 'Early socialisation and its long-term effects on adult behaviour in dogs', *Journal of Veterinary Behaviour*, 5(2), pp. 51-59. DOI: 10.1016/j.jveb.2010.03.002.

Vanand, M., et al. (2020). *Maternal diabetes and its impact on offspring health in dogs: A review of current findings.* Veterinary Journal, 258, 105442. https://doi.org/10.1016/j.tvjl.2020.105442

Waller, B.M. and Caeiro, C. (2013) 'Assessing emotional responses in domestic dogs through vocal and body signals', Animal Behaviour, 86, pp. 285-293. doi:10.1016/j.anbehav.2013.05.005

Wilson, C. and Davison, G. (2006) 'The impact of early social experiences on canine behaviour', *Applied Animal Behaviour Science*, 100(3-4), pp. 278-288. DOI: 10.1016/j.applanim.2006.07.001.

Wright, J. (2018). *The importance of socialization in puppy development.* Journal of Veterinary Behaviour, 28, 1-7. https://doi.org/10.1016/j.jveb.2018.01.002

Wysong, T. (2008). *Canine Nutrition: A Nutritional Guide for Dog Owners.* Wysong Corporation.

Zanghi, B.M. and Rodda, G.H. (2013) 'Maternal care and its effect on offspring behaviour in domestic dogs', *Journal of Veterinary Behaviour*, 8(4), pp. 229-235. doi:10.1016/j.jveb.2013.08.002